GW00630676

1982

THE SINGLEHANDERS

THE SINGLEHANDERS

Peter Heaton

HASTINGS HOUSE, PUBLISHERS: NEW YORK

(Previous pages) **Francis Chichester, visible on the extreme left, rounds Cape Horn during his solo circumnavigation, March 1967**

Published in U.S.A. October, 1976
by Hastings House, Publishers, Inc.
First published in 1976 in England by Michael Joseph Ltd, London

© 1976 by Peter Heaton

Library of Congress Cataloging in Publication Data
Heaton, Peter, 1919-
The singlehanders.
Bibliography: p. 204-5
1. Sailing. I. Title.
GV811.H3565   797.1'24   76-8423
ISBN 0-8038-6735-2

Designed and produced by London Editions Limited, 30 Uxbridge Road, London W12 8ND

Printed and bound in Great Britain by
Chromoworks Ltd, Nottingham
and Dorstel Press Ltd, Harlow

CONTENTS

PROLOGUE
Singlehanders' talk

God's clock is not the same as our clock. He has an
infinite amount of our time. Ours has very nearly run
out.[1]   The only time I feel lonely is when in harbour
surrounded by noisy and anonymous crowds.[2]
Somehow I never seemed to enjoy so much doing
things with other people.[3]   I am not happy on
land.[4]   A life which is damnably dull is not worth the
living.[5]   Sailing the Atlantic alone is really dreadfully
boring.[6]   My voyage . . . was my way of seeing some
interesting parts of the world.[7]   As far as I was
concerned I wasn't taking any great risks.[8]   I think a
man would have to be inhumanly confident and self-
reliant if he were to make this sort of voyage without
faith in God.[9]   When I was five years old I knew all
about God.[10]   I have no desire to return to Europe
with all its false gods.[11]   During his life time each
man plays cosmic chess against the Devil.[12]   I am
delighted to say that . . . he found me distressingly
normal.[13]   To me ships were something in which one
crossed the sea in order to get to the other side.[14]   I
was sailing round the world simply because I bloody
well wanted to.[15]   Recently there have been a
number of loose claims for distances and speeds
sailed.[16]   The trans-Pacific race . . . is a good test of
stamina.[17]   I am longing for the sea, I implore you to
take me with you.[18]   I felt myself an insect on a straw
in the midst of the elements.[19]   I wanted to be that
Briton.[20]   I wanted to survive the ultimate, the
knock-down![21]   I achieved great calmness.[22]   To
look at life for a little while from a new
perspective.[23]   Oh 'tis 'orrible to be out, matey.
Mountaineous seas, eighteen inches high an' horrible
great black clouds.[24]   The frequency of the gales
appalled me.[25]   I have felt a community with dead
seamen on many occasions.[26]   I do not do a thing
nearly as well when with someone.[27]   Don't think
I'm crazy. I am in very good health.[28]   There is

something almost sacred about boat building.[29] I'm very disappointed in the boat, she's not right, I'm not prepared.[30] I am going because I would have no peace if I stayed.[31] As for myself the wonderful sea charmed me from the first.[32] God how good it is to live like an animal.[33] Loneliness . . . can take you close to Hell and sometimes, just sometimes, close to Heaven.[34] I am always roving in quest of youth.[35] Planking is quite an exciting part of building a boat.[36] Solid, simple, sure; and fast on all points of sailing.[37] *Whilst a' sailin' the* Sunday Times *race; I sublimate sexual urgesses: by sailing a Clipper ship pace; an' a' writin' o' dirty vergesses.*[38] I wanted to see more distant lands in a vessel of my own.[39] I am no longer frightened of meeting men.[40] The voyage was something I simply *had* to do.[41] Make money, make money; to do what? To change your car when it is still going well? To dress decently . . . to have television?[42] If ever I dream, I'll dream of this storm.[43] Why not sail round the world the other way?[44] A sailor has no business to be lonely.[45] I sailed to prove to myself that I could, that is enough. I don't see what it would prove to go again.[46]

[1]*Donald Crowhurst* [2]*Michael Mermod* [3]*Francis Chichester* [4]*Alain Gerbault* [5]*J. P. Magnan* [6]*Nicolette Coward* [7]*Harry Pidgeon* [8]*Robert Manry* [9]*Robin Knox-Johnston* [10]*Donald Crowhurst* [11]*Bernard Moitessier* [12]*Donald Crowhurst* [13]*Robin Knox-Johnston* [14]*Ann Davison* [15]*Robin Knox-Johnston* [16]*Francis Chichester* [17]*Eric Tabarly* [18]letter written to *Alain Gerbault* [19]*Joshua Slocum* [20]*Robin Knox-Johnston* [21]*Alec Rose* [22]*Alain Colas* [23]*Robert Manry* [24]*Donald Crowhurst* [25]*Robin Knox-Johnston* [26]*Donald Crowhurst* [27]*Francis Chichester* [28]*Bernard Moitessier* [29]*John Guzzwell* [30,31]*Donald Crowhurst* [32]*Joshua Slocum* [33]*Bernard Moitessier* [34]*Robin Lee Graham* [35]*Alain Gerbault* [36]*Donald Ridler* [37]*Bernard Moitessier* [38]*Donald Crowhurst* [39]*Harry Pidgeon* [40]*Bernard Moitessier* [41]*Robert Manry* [42]*Bernard Moitessier* [43]*Chay Blyth* [44]*Maureen Blyth* [45]*Rob Roy MacGregor* [46]*Marie Claude Fauroux*

'There is nothing to escape from
And nothing to escape to. One is always alone.'

T. S. ELIOT

THE BOREDOM of daily repetitious work! Trapped like an animal, not by wire and stake, but by steel and concrete, by rules, regulations, tax-forms, crowds, petty officials, timetables and all the trivia of life, especially urban life! To all wearying under these irritations, the idea of sailing a boat across oceans, free of all restrictions save those set by nature, free to sail on any point of the compass to virtually any horizon, must always be a dream to set the pulse racing.

And perhaps especially to do it alone, singlehanded!

There have been quite a number of very long singlehanded yacht passages in recent years, including several circumnavigations. They have been written about, filmed, televised, and there has been much comment, both favourable and condemnatory. The latter includes that which holds it to be a self-indulgent enterprise largely for fame and monetary reward, liable to put the lives of rescuers at risk and to waste money generally. Certainly the welcome given to Sir Francis Chichester when a quarter of a million people waited for him at Plymouth Hoe, the TV appearances, and the subsequent best-selling book had opened up possibilities in recent years. But neither money nor fame provided the motivation for this extraordinary man. There were plenty of solo circumnavigators prior to Chichester, and as we shall see there are a variety of reasons why people go voyaging alone in a yacht. 'I wanted to survive the ultimate, the knock-down!' This from quiet deceptively gentle-mannered Sir Alec Rose, knighted after his singlehanded circumnavigation of the world in 1967-8, and coming from a man who admits to a 'vivid imagination', is a fascinating admission. Surely one of the most extraordinary reasons for going singlehanded off-shore! Being 'knocked-down' is sufficiently unpleasant to deter most people capable of visualizing it from wanting to experience it at first hand. The overcoming of fear, winning the battle with the sea, clearly played a strong part in Alec Rose's motivation, but to go to sea deliberately

(Previous pages) **Another British singlehander, Alec Rose, who like Chichester sailed round the world with one stop and home to a knighthood, in the 36ft Calcutta-built** 'Lively Lady'

looking for one of the more nightmarish situations is what? Masochistic? French tennis player and Riviera playboy, Alain Gerbault, suddenly abandoned the hedonist's way of life to go singlehanded sailing. Gerbault said that his long solo passages were ' . . . only for the fun of the thing' and to prove he could do it '. . . all alone . . .' His experiences on his first Atlantic crossing in the cutter *Firecrest* could not be described as 'fun' by the most masochistic seafarer. However, the remark came after the crossing was well behind him. Gerbault, who described himself as '. . . always roving in quest of youth . . .', was a more complex personality than the self-admitted 'dreamer' Alec Rose.

John Caldwell did it for love. He made a 9000-mile Pacific Ocean passage singlehanded simply because it was the only way to get to the young bride he had left in Australia. Stuck in Panama with no ship available, he acquired a yacht, set off, and taught himself navigation on the way!

A much more recent singlehander, Peter Woolass, took up solo sailing partly through shortage of crew and found that it suited his temperament; but he also admits that to make a solo ocean crossing was a dream of long standing.

Robin Lee Graham, who in 1965 made singlehander history by his epic 'voyage round the world' when only sixteen years old, said that he was prompted by '. . . the same desire to get out of the rut . . . to prove perhaps that a kid doesn't have to be boxed in until he is a mental and spiritual dummy in a business suit . . .'

The irascible Victorian pioneer of small boat cruising, Richard McMullen, came originally to singlehanded sailing when he dismissed his two paid hands because they were 'idle and insolent'. He then sailed the yacht *Orion* home singlehanded; thus, in the words of Frank Cowper, establishing his claim to be '. . . the first to show how one man could handle a large boat'. One wonders what he would have thought of Jean-Yves Terlain's huge schooner *Vendredi XIII*. McMullen, as hard on himself as he was on others, took to solo sailing, sometimes in minute vessels, and from his writing it is evident that the standards he set for seamanship were so high that rather than put up with the indifferent crews who infuriated him so much, he preferred to sail alone. It is also clear that he thoroughly enjoyed it.

But if McMullen got pleasure from sailing singlehanded

a vessel normally requiring a crew, so did Sir Francis Chichester. Chichester, though, was also a racing enthusiast and his motivation was partly the challenge involved in sailing the various *Gypsy Moths* as fast as possible. He was a born singlehander, who admitted that he did not '. . . do a thing nearly as well when with someone'. Whether flying or sailing, Chichester knew that he was at his best alone.

One of the most interesting of recent circumnavigators is French intellectual Bernard Moitessier. In the *Sunday Times* sponsored non-stop round-the-world singlehanded race of 1968-9, Moitessier was in a favourable position and could have been the winner. In choosing to sail on round the Cape of Good Hope to the Indian Ocean for a second time instead of finishing the course, he effectively demonstrated his indifference to the fame awaiting the winner. The true singlehander, says Moitessier, sails for the love of the sea and sailing. His mysticism, his belief in the spiritual value of lone sailing, comes out in his book *The Long Way*—whose royalties he gave away.

It is certainly not necessarily for money or lionization, then, that this singlehander sails. But other solo yachtsmen admit quite cheerfully that they like the adulation. The attractive Nicolette Milnes-Walker (now Mrs Coward) —who happens to be a trained psychologist—was quite frank about enjoying the fame that being the first woman to make the non-stop crossing of the Atlantic Ocean brought her.

Donald Ridler, who made a solo crossing of the Atlantic in a boat he built in the back garden of his father's rectory, seems deliberately to have made his task harder. For not only did he build the boat in which he made his passage, he built her incredibly cheaply—for only £165 ($400) with another £90 ($220) for her gear. When he started building, his ideas went no further than home waters, but while building he was made the subject of humorous enquiries as to whether he was going to sail across the Atlantic, and the taunt provided the challenge. Ridler's motivation for his crossing appears to have been 'Well, why not?' as much as anything, but it is more likely that he wanted to prove that he could do it. He wrote an excellent book about his feat, as did many of the people we shall be discussing.

Another who built his own boat was lone circumnavigator John Guzzwell. There could hardly be two more

Cape Horn weather reducing the sail plan of Francis Chichester's sleek and swift 'Gypsy Moth IV' **to storm jib, on the first-ever single-handed circumnavigation with one stop (Sydney)** en route

different attitudes to the task than those of Ridler and Guzzwell. Ridler's description is laconic, matter-of-fact. The nearest he gets to the romantic idea is when he admits that '. . . planking is quite an exciting part of building a boat'. The tough circumnavigator Guzzwell, on the other hand, felt that there was something '. . . almost sacred' about boat building. It is, he says, rather like 'creating a living being'. Guzzwell's boat *Trekka* was one of the smallest ever to have made a very long distance passage, being only 18ft 6in. on the water line. In this minute vessel he sailed around the world alone. He set off for Hawaii in company with another yacht, *Tzu Hang*, sailed by a retired Indian Army brigadier and his family. While in New Zealand waters Guzzwell shipped temporarily with Smeeton (the brigadier) as additional crew, and experienced a remarkable 'knock-down' in the South Pacific near Cape Horn in which the vessel was turned stern over bows. Under jury rig they managed to reach Chile, and their story is a subject of a book by Miles Smeeton entitled *Once is Enough. (*In practice, for Smeeton it wasn't!)

The terrifying experience of being turned over by a freak wave in no way inhibited John Guzzwell either. May 1956 found him off again in *Trekka* to complete his circumnavigation, returning to Victoria, British Columbia, on 12 September 1959, having sailed 33,000 miles. It had taken him four years and two days to do it. Guzzwell's passage was full of friendly interludes. He hardly seems like a typical singlehander, yet he admits it was the prospect of sailing 'alone' that he found so particularly satisfying.

A solo voyage which ended in tragedy was that of Donald Crowhurst. He entered the trimaran *Teignmouth Electron* in the *Sunday Times* non-stop round-the-world race which was won by Robin Knox-Johnston. Crowhurst, self-styled an 'incurable romantic', had conducted a strenuous campaign to raise the money for a yacht to sail round the world non-stop. Initially he had tried to persuade the Cutty Sark Society to allow him to sail Francis Chichester's *Gypsy Moth IV*, but the former thought it better that Chichester's famous boat should be housed in a dry dock at Greenwich as originally planned.

Undaunted, Crowhurst succeeded in finding a backer, and the trimaran was built and launched, but when the time came to sail, he was far from happy with the boat. On the evening of his departure he was in a state of nervous tension, suffering from lack of sleep. But Crowhurst had in fact been built up by a publicity campaign, and by now his enterprise had its own momentum. Perhaps one half of him knew he should not go, should back out while there was still time, and who knows how far the other had been seduced by thoughts of being a popular hero? His failure is one of the sea's tragedies, as emerges in a later chapter. It is also one of the sea's mysteries, but one thing is certain: he exhibited considerable courage in his own way and although his voyage, as we shall see, was a deception, those who would decry him do not fully appreciate the problem.

The early singlehanders, like Slocum, Blackburn, Gerbault, Dumas, Gau, McMullen, Graham etc. did not race, but since five men—Chichester, Val Howells, David Lewis, Jean Lacombe and Colonel 'Blondie' Hasler—raced solo across the Atlantic in 1960, the fashion has spread. The first race, the idea for which came from Colonel Hasler, a very experienced ocean racing man, was sponsored by the *Observer* newspaper, and there have been several since, with the interest and numbers increasing. Thus in 1960, there were five; in 1964, fifteen; in 1968, thirty-five, and fifty-nine in 1972. This last race was a very international affair, and the entry list contained single-handers from America, Australia, France, Belgium, West Germany, Italy, Poland and Czechoslovakia; there were also widely differing types and sizes of craft. Final placings showed that first, second and third place had been taken by three Frenchmen. A tragic sequence was the retirement through ill health of the gallant Sir Francis Chichester.

The racing element is not approved by some singlehanders, and not everyone would agree with French yachting hero Eric Tabarly's maxim that you do not just cross the ocean, you drive the boat at her fastest every centimetre of the way. Tabarly is a most persistent devotee of ocean racing. His attractive singlehander compatriot, Marie-Claude Fauroux, admitted that she had sailed the 1972 race to prove to herself that she could; that was enough. 'I don't see', she said, 'what it would prove to go again.'

The motives which drive this or that yachtsman to sail further than his fellows are in essence no different from those which send men up mountains or deep into jungles. Take the example of singlehander Sir Alec Rose. He admits that part of his motivation was a wish to experience at first hand what it was like to be 'knocked-down' by a big

Peering pensively from a hatchway, French singlehanded yachtsman, author and romantic, Alain Gerbault, looks towards the stern of 'Firecrest', anchored at St Vincent, Cape Verde Islands

sea—a wish to sail a ship in the violent waters of the Southern Ocean. He was deliberately giving himself a challenge, setting out to do something he knew would probably frighten him (it takes a good deal of courage to sail a boat in the Roaring Forties, and we will examine the reasons in Chapter 6) because he wanted to prove to himself that he could rise above it. Rose is a most relaxed person to meet, modest and with a personal magnetism that goes far beyond mere charm of manner. No-one would deny that the early circumnavigation of his was a very remarkable achievement. His drive was certainly partly personal, that is to say, self-achievement to produce a sense of having acquired great self-respect through attainment. The more arduous the task the greater the self-respect.

For many people it is harder to understand why these individuals would wish so particularly to do it 'alone'. It would seem that part of the answer lies in independence, part in self-achievement. (This is greater if by doing it 'alone' the achievement is more.) Sir Alec Rose has described the typical singlehander as ' . . . a sort of dark horse . . . a dreamer, an idealist and individualist'. He was answering the question 'Why alone?', and although his words convey a certain type of man they do not answer the question.

When we come to consider the motive of escapism we have, say, in the person of Bernard Moitessier, a man who is frustrated by the world of urban man. He rationalizes that by keeping at sea 'away from it all', by opting out of 'life in Europe', he can compensate for all the frustration of that misguided continent. Moitessier wrote that he was no longer 'frightened of meeting men', but he did not particularly want to meet any! He felt his long periods in the Southern Ocean had changed him and, in his opinion, for the better. Things which had been very important to him before had ceased to count. It was good, he said, ' . . . to live like an animal'. Moitessier, a very experienced sailor, has written several classics on sailing the seas.

But what of women singlehanders—people like Ann Davison, who sailed the Atlantic in the early 1950s and was the first woman to make such a crossing singlehanded? Her husband had been drowned earlier while they were sailing together. One would have understood if Mrs Davison had had no further wish to sail in a yacht; yet she did, and did it alone. Another remarkable solo sailor is Mrs Sharon

Adams, the first woman to sail the 6000 miles from Japan to San Diego; an immense distance for anyone to sail singlehanded.

We shall later consider the competitive element in singlehanded sailing, the racing element. One who disagrees with this is Australian Bill Howell, known as 'Tahiti Bill', who maintains that the true singlehander is not competitive. Howell has taken part in racing, but he sails for the sake of sailing and he enjoys sailing alone. The idea of singlehanded racing did not catch on immediately, and Lady Chichester recalls how little interested the American press was in the first singlehanded race across the Atlantic. The British press decided, she said, that 'Americans like togetherness and we like alone-with-it-all.' But that was racing. There have been great American singlehanders since Nova Scotian Joshua Slocum's *Spray* carried the stars and stripes around the world. People like Alfred Johnson and Harry Pidgeon are part of singlehander history, and Pidgeon adds his own quote to the 'alone' problem: 'My voyage', he said, 'was not undertaken for the joy of sailing alone. It was my way of seeing some interesting parts of the world.'

There is one aspect of singlehanded sailing that most people can imagine, however ignorant they may be of the effects of bad weather, and that is the effect of loneliness. Clearly to some singlehanders it was of little account, but in other cases it became a very real, even sinister factor. Even Slocum, old hand that he was, wrote when in fog and rising gale, 'The waves rose high . . . in the dismal fog I felt myself drifting into loneliness, an insect on a straw in the midst of the elements.' The early singlehanders had no radio contact with the world. They were truly alone, whereas nowadays the modern lone sailor has increasing radio technology at his elbow. Yet it is still very easy to become lost. In the vastness of the Southern Ocean Donald Crowhurst was able to hide from all shipping while the other 'Golden Globe' contestants sailed round the world.

In such huge spaces of ocean a yacht, radio-equipped or not, is truly on her own and loneliness can become a thing of menace. The seeds of poor Crowhurst's deterioration may have already been in him, but solitude played its part. It is true he had some radio contact with his sponsors and his wife, but all singlehanders agree that loneliness is greatest just after the termination of such a contact. It is

Controversial globe-wanderer, expert seaman: French yachtsman Bernard Moitessier adjusts 'Joshua's' warps at the quayside of Papeete, in the island of Tahiti

then that silence is most felt, solitude most tangible. To die alone at sea is a terrible thing and even the prospect of it is daunting. In 1974 the well-known French circumnavigator Alain Colas experienced real terror for two days, produced by loneliness and nothing else in the desolate waters near Cape Horn. The singlehander exhibits a particular kind of courage.

In a first-class book, called *The Ulysses Factor*, yachtsman and writer John Anderson has analysed the special combination of qualities that make up this factor. Taking the hero as his starting point, Anderson concerns himself with the study of a continuing quality in mankind: a quality which leads to 'the cool taking advantage of calculated risks'. But even if we allow that a particular type of adventurous courage provides the source of many a singlehander's drive, there are plenty of people who hold that the solo sailor is just escaping from the necessary restrictions of civilized society, from everyday life, and escaping selfishly. A remark made to the writer recently was to the effect that all a person like Moitessier really wanted was an irresponsible freedom from the restraint of civilized life.

Freedom from restraint. Man has always loved freedom, but it has taken him a long time to bring it within his grasp. Wild men in the dawn of history may be said to have enjoyed more freedom than their town-dwelling, civilized successors, but they had their own form of oppression in the shape of lack of food, disease and, perhaps particularly, their own ignorance and fear. As these basic threats to freedom gradually diminished, and men came to live in villages and towns, other threats to the freedom of the ordinary man were to appear, one being in the form of serfdom. Although they could be said to possess a fair degree of freedom, yet for centuries the mass of the people have had to live lives in which their waking hours were spent, originally under constraint, dominated and ruled by those in power, and later under the continual pressure of the machine age after the industrial revolution. Such people knew little of personal freedom, yet it is the machine which has changed everything.

Of course there is still plenty of inequality in the world today, but if one can take Britain as an example, the majority of people are educated and not ignorant; properly fed and not hungry; with money to spend and freedom to spend it. The pattern may be seen all over the world. Today this revolutionary change in the structure of society, this expansion of freedom for the individual, has produced its own problems. Such freedom would have been unbelievable to a person like the stockbroker yachtsman, Richard McMullen. Today a man has a fair chance of reaching whatever heights he is capable of, without having to surmount the barriers of, say, Victorian England; and furthermore can exercise his critical faculties to a very marked degree. Those forms of society which for a long time have been dominated by elites have always been governed according to a set code of morality. It has been necessary to conform. In the more permissive societies of the modern world a new code is substituted, a new morality, that of freedom. It is this new personal freedom combined with no firm moral order that is causing much of the confusion in modern society. Those against the permissive society view it askance as an order without restraint. Those who support the new order point out that in it the burden is on personal responsibility; with freedom comes responsibility.

The argument that the singlehanded sailor is merely escaping from restraint also implies that his actions are irresponsible and misguided in that true personal freedom goes a long way beyond life without restraint. 'Living' means living with, and influencing, others and being influenced by them. But it is not as if the singlehander is away at sea for most of his life; his voyages are generally interludes in an otherwise perfectly normal existence, and the preparation for a long voyage involves many people. It has been said too that the lone sailor loses touch with reality. Certainly striving under modern conditions of stress can easily induce the desire to escape into a world of fantasy. Several of the singlehanders have confessed to wishing to prolong the voyage; to feeling deflated and empty at its conclusion; and to an aversion to come to grips again with the bustling world.

Being alone for a long time requires adjustment. Having got accustomed to it, some of those who find solitude of value quite naturally find it distasteful to relinquish a hard-won peace of mind and tranquillity. Life has temporarily been reduced to simple essentials: the kind of simplicity that, if one is wise, one plans for that longed-for holiday from office routine. To stress the escapist factor is to misunderstand the singlehanded sailor. Certainly he appreciates solitude. The American journalist Robert Manry, who sailed the Atlantic in the 13½ft dinghy *Tinkerbelle*, is on record as saying that his voyage enabled him to '. . . stand back, away from human society ashore, and look at life for a little while from a new perspective.'

Ever since Chichester, the long singlehanded voyage has become almost fashionable. There had been plenty of circumnavigations in yachts before *Gypsy Moth IV*, but not with only one stop. Moreover, Chichester had a flair for catching the public imagination. He had style. It has been suggested that the extraordinary emotive interest which his voyage aroused in the British public was due to a desire, in the absence of funds to finance astronauts, to prove that a British adventurer could still 'show the world', and that Chichester, with his special combination of reserve and panache, was just the man to do it. There may or may not be something in this, but is quite certain that one result of such voyages as those of Chichester and Alec Rose was to fire a number of adventurous young men with a determination to follow in their wake. The difficulty was how to go 'one better'. The *Sunday Times* non-stop race was one answer, yet in the middle of it, the Frenchman, Moitessier, who had almost reached the home stretch, was to show his considered disapproval by breaking off the race to continue a second time round the world rather than return to Europe to 'have a television' and to be '. . . pushed, forced, ordered about . . . by false gods'.

But quite apart from the competitive factor, there is also strong motivation from the love of adventure and of the sea and seafaring. First pioneer Joshua Slocum's spiritual successor, Robin Knox-Johnston, has said that the library of books he took with him contained twenty-five on the sea and sea-life because (like Slocum) the whole subject fascinated him. Knox-Johnston, an experienced sailor, has a thoroughly practical approach. The *Sunday Mirror* (with whom he had a writing contract) sent him to a psychiatrist in order that a comparison could be made between his two mental states pre- and post-voyage. On both occasions he was found to be 'distressingly normal'.

Knox-Johnston, admitting that he was doing nothing to advance scientific knowledge (by comparison, for example, with the astronauts), was determined, now that Chichester and Rose had shown global circumnavigation to be possible, that the first to do it 'non-stop' must be a Briton. 'I wanted', he admits, 'to be that Briton.' But patriotism was not the only reason. His mother had dubbed the voyage 'totally irresponsible', and Knox-Johnston half admitted that she was right. He was sailing alone round the world '. . . simply because I bloody well wanted to'. He adds that he was thoroughly enjoying himself.

Another singlehander who invites comparison with Knox-Johnston is Scots ex-paratrooper Chay Blyth. They are much the same age, Knox-Johnston being twenty-nine and Blyth thirty at the time of their voyages. They both circumnavigated the globe without stopping, and both had service-training—Knox-Johnston in the Merchant Navy and Blyth in the Paratroop Regiment. There were three major differences. First, Blyth was not competing in any race, secondly, he did not have Knox-Johnston's seaman's training, and thirdly, his ship *British Steel*, sponsored by the British Steel Coporation, was nearly twice as large as Knox-Johnston's *Suhaili*, and was designed and built specially for the purpose.

However, the significant thing about Blyth's voyage is that he sailed round the world the 'wrong way round'. This phrase requires some explanation. In making a complete circumnavigation, the sailor will eventually find himself (because of the intervening land masses of the continents) south of latitude 40° South. A glance at the map of wind systems will show why. In this part, the 'Roaring Forties', where there is very little intervening land, there is nothing to check the sea and swell that has been moving since the dawn of this planet. The prevailing winds blow strongly and they blow from the west. So the ships of the days of sail, taking advantage of this, sailed eastwards round the Cape of Good Hope, eastwards to Australia and, eventually, eastwards round the Horn. To sail westwards round the Horn, westwards to New Zealand and Australia and westwards to the Cape of Good Hope, to go against the prevailing system all the way—and not only the winds, the accompanying seas and swell—is to make the passage doubly difficult.

When Knox-Johnston was first considering sailing round the world he realized that the only way left to do it was 'non-stop'. Both Chichester and Rose had done it with one stop. For Chay Blyth the question was how to go one better, which he needed to do for his own satisfaction. Back

in 1967 he left the army, and in 1968 he was going to enter for the singlehanded trans-Atlantic race of that year. He changed his mind and decided to take part in the *Sunday Times* race round the world. During this he disqualified himself by putting into harbour in South Africa.

While in South Africa he had met an old friend, a fellow Scot and former paratrooper. Together they discussed the possibility of crossing the Andes and navigating the whole of the Amazon River by canoe. It was an idea that particularly appealed to Blyth, especially at a time when he was obsessed by a sense of failure. He thought a lot about it, but he gave equal thought to a chance remark made by his wife Maureen who, to make him laugh and lift him from a fit of depression, had said '. . . why not sail round the world the other way?' The more he thought about it, the more he liked it. How he, a retired soldier with no money, brought it off, we shall see later. For the present we are concerned solely with the fact that Blyth's motivation was partly the lure of high adventure and endeavour and partly to wipe out a failure—as had, in its way, been Donald Crowhurst's voyage. Blyth, in his excellent book *The Impossible Voyage,* is understanding and generous in his reference to Crowhurst's tragic voyage. Blyth had a tough passage, as was to be expected, and he had his fair share of problems.

A yachtsman who sometimes sails with a crew and sometimes sails singlehanded is Frenchman Eric Tabarly. As legendary in his own way as his fellow countryman Moitessier, Tabarly has become something of a god to the French ocean-racing fraternity. For with Tabarly, the main motivation for sailing is to race. Everything is subordinated to 'getting home first', to 'winning'. When he sails solo, his object is the same. If it is a 'solo' race, he enters—to win the race. An example of this is the first trans-Pacific race from San Francisco to Tokyo. Tabarly entered the yacht *Pen Duick V*, a very light displacement vessel which was built for the race, and won it. The other competitors were Jean-Yves Terlain, also French, Claus Hehner, a German, Belgian René Hauwaert and American Jerry Cartwright.

Tabarly has had a spectacularly successful off-shore racing career. He is tremendously involved in the design and development of racing boats and in *Pen Duick II* (the first *Pen Duick* was his father's) he won the 1964 trans-Atlantic race. In *Pen Duick III*, a schooner-rigged vessel

No longer a male preserve, singlehanded sailing has benefited from the advent of girls like the French Marie Claude Fauroux, as good-looking as she is competent

25

57ft in length, he chalked up victories in the classic ocean races of the world such as the British Fastnet and the Australian Sydney-Hobart. *Pen Duick IV*, his next development, was a 68ft aluminium trimaran (three-hulled like Crowhurst's *Teignmouth Electron*). His attempt in the 1968 trans-Atlantic (the race Chay Blyth abandoned to try for the Round-the-World *Sunday Times* race) was a failure owing to a collision with a merchant ship. But later *Pen Duick IV* was to cut almost twenty-four hours off the time for a passage from Los Angeles to Honolulu. *Pen Duick V*, as already noted, was designed to win the first singlehanded race across the Pacific; and she did. Of the trans-Pacific race, Tabarly said there is much to recommend it, being long and necessitating much sail changing. It is a 'good test of stamina'; nevertheless Tabarly has stated that it is not as 'hard a race as the trans-Atlantic' because of the prevalence of bad weather and windward sailing in the latter.

There are many similarities between Eric Tabarly and Francis Chichester, in that both were motivated by the desire to compete and win in challenging conditions. But while Chichester openly confessed to a great preference for being 'alone', to Tabarly it does not appear to matter. The attraction of solo sailing seems to him to be simply that without a crew it is that much harder! Perhaps there is an even greater similarity between Chichester and another immensely experienced French singlehander, Alain Colas. In 1974 Colas circumnavigated the world with one stop to clip Chichester's time by fifty-seven days. Colas too is a racing singlehander, a competitor.

Clearly, it is the challenge of racing alone that motivates some singlehanders. With others it is purely the love of adventure, and with others again, a love of the sea and of the peace of mind which comes from lone sailing and taking on the sea in all weathers alone. It is not for money. Over and again men have bankrupted themselves to build a boat and sail her over the horizon. It is the challenge that motivates above all, but it is more than mere adventure. It is an expression of the vital spirit in mankind which in a few leads to positive action. The challenge comes in many guises but there is no mistaking the genuine, as opposed to what Erskine Childers (in *The Riddle of the Sands*) called the 'bastard concoction' of Bohemian or urban life. Mankind needs challenges, and if the example of the singlehanders serves to remind us of the vital importance of high adventure and of adversity met with cheerful courage, their voyages are anything but useless, selfish exercises in romantic escapism. To those of us who live in overcrowded cities, the escapist theory may seem at first both plausible and understandable; but not on reflection, when one considers the hardship involved over long periods. The singlehander's escapist dream, if that is all it is, has got to stand up to months of cold, wet, lack of sleep and loneliness, interspersed by periods of fear. It can be a dangerous as well as unnerving experience to sail alone into the far oceans.

To be carried out successfully, the sort of enterprises we have been talking about require effort and skill. How much? And how dangerous, in fact, are they? Is it not selfish to hazard the lifeboats and their crews and all the rescue services, and a misuse of public money? Again, is it not selfish to leave wives, homes and families behind in the pursuit of this form of pleasure? And how do the wives feel about it? Do women sail singlehanded or is it a male preserve? Do some people set forth who should be stopped? Is it possible to be unbalanced by solitude? Has not more than one voyage ended in stark tragedy? The next chapter begins our enquiry.

A SEARCH for the first singlehanders reveals many interesting facts and some fiction. Probably fictitious, certainly unsubstantiated, is the claim of Captain Cleveland of Salem, Massachusetts, to have crossed the Indian and Pacific Oceans singlehanded in a 15ft boat in 1800. In 1849 J. M. Cranston sailed the 41ft *Toccao* from New Bedford to San Francisco; some 13,000 miles in 226 days. Although the voyage is verifiable from the New Bedford *Evening Standard*, it also reveals that Cranston had a crew. He was not alone. Turning towards the American sea-board fishing grounds of the North Atlantic, however, we come upon an indisputable singlehander.

The first man on record to sail the Atlantic singlehanded was Alfred Johnson, a Grand Banks fisherman. His boat was called *Centennial* and 1876, the year of his voyage, was the hundredth anniversary of the United States of America. She was a type of small fishing vessel known as a dory and only 20ft in length. In this diminutive craft, rigged for the voyage as a gaff cutter, Johnson crossed the great western ocean, arriving in Pembrokeshire, Wales, after a passage of sixty-four days.

The passage was not an easy one. After trouble with his compass, which for a navigator is like an athlete having something amiss with his heart, Johnson finally got away on 22 June. In spite of some minor damage and a lot of water below decks, he weathered his first gale without mishap. The winds were favourable, strong south-westerlies blowing him swiftly on his course throughout the month of July. He had had the foresight to carry a squaresail in addition to the usual working sails of a cutter, and he was able to put the big rectangle of canvas, set at right-angles to the boat, to good use.

It was at the beginning of August that his troubles began. *Centennial* was within three hundred miles of the nearest point of the Irish coast, and the crossing must have seemed almost over. The wind increased steadily and big seas began to build up. Johnson reduced sail. The weather continued to worsen, and he hove to, adjusting the reefed sails to ride out the gale without making any forward progress. This takes much of the sting out of the wind's force, but if it really blows up there are times when heaving-to is not sufficient. Johnson decided to unship his

(Previous pages) **R. T. McMullen's 'Orion' in which, having dismissed his crew for insolence, he made a singlehanded passage from France to England—not far as distance goes, but the vessel was a large one with heavy gear. This probably gave McMullen a taste for later solo passages**

mast, which in the conditions that must have prevailed at the time was an action bordering on the heroic. But he managed it and safely lashed the mast and its gear down on deck.

To the exhausted man, it must have seemed the final blow from fate when, in the afternoon, the little *Centennial* was turned right over by a giant sea, and lay there bottom upwards. Having no outside iron or lead ballast to help right her, there was no reason why she should not float bottom upwards as well as bottom downwards, and on the top, stretched across the keel, lay Alfred Johnson! For more than a quarter of an hour he clung there. How he managed to get his boat the right way up is hard to visualize. But he did, and bailed her out, and all the time and throughout the night the gale continued its full force.

The morning brought some moderation in the weather and Johnson was able to take stock of the situation. Amongst a lot of gear which had fallen out of the boat in the capsize was his paraffin stove; he had therefore no way to cook any food, neither could he dry out his clothes and bedding which—like his food—was of course all saturated. The conditions under which he now managed to get sailing again are difficult to imagine. He must have had a tremendously strong will to survive. On 7 August, the brig *Alfredon* sighted him. She came alongside and put bread and fresh water on board *Centennial*. Two days later he was able to find out his position, some fifty-three miles west by south of Wexford Head, when the *Prince Lombardo*, another ship, gave it to him. He eventually arrived off the Welsh coast near Milford Haven, having missed Ireland altogether, and sailed into Abercastle in Pembrokeshire after being at sea for sixty-four days.

One might well think that Johnson would now wish to rest and recuperate, but not he! After only two days, he sailed up the Irish Sea to Holyhead and Liverpool. It had originally been his intention to have his boat shipped back to America (after a successful crossing) in order that she might form part of the Great Exhibition at Philadelphia to mark the hundredth anniversary of the United States.

However, although his voyage had taken too long for this to be done, his place in sailing history is assured. He was a plain sailor-man and his boat was basically a simple dory, only 20ft long. He had sailed singlehanded across the great western ocean, from North America to the British Isles, a distance of 2835 miles, something no-one had ever done before. And it must surely rank as one of the toughest small boat voyages ever made.

If Alfred Johnson deserves his place for his endurance and the magnitude of his feat of seamanship, there is yet another pioneer who as surely rates his place in our account for other reasons. Rob Roy MacGregor's voyage, alone in the yawl which bore his name, pre-dated Alfred Johnson's feat in *Centennial* by nine years. Yet it is not the cruise that earns MacGregor his mention here, for by comparison it was insignificant, but the man who made it.

John 'Rob Roy' MacGregor was the sort of man who naturally attracts and holds the limelight. He was called 'Rob Roy' as a child and took the name as his trademark in later years. John's father, Duncan MacGregor, was a soldier and saw much service. Rob Roy's education was thus typical of many children of serving soldiers: attending, as the family followed his father's postings, eight different schools, including the King's School, Canterbury. Eventually, after attending both Dublin College and Trinity College Cambridge, Rob Roy left twenty-fourth Wrangler (i.e. with a first class Honours Degree in mathematics), and came to London reasonably pleased with himself and intending to read for the Bar.

To his natural intelligence was added a lively if not formidable capacity for adventure! He was in Paris during the Revolution of 1848 and in the following year began the first of his foreign travels, making a journey to Greece, Turkey, Syria, Egypt and Palestine. His interests were inexhaustible. In May 1853 he was able to write:

> . . . among the objects now claiming my best attention are the Protestant Alliance, the Protestant Defence Society, the Ragged School Union, the Shoeblacks, the Ragged School Shop, the Band of Hope Review, the True Briton, the Town Mission, the Open Air Mission, the Slavery Question, the Preventative and Reformatory School Society, the Lawyer's Prayer Union and the Mansfield Society.

A record of his physical activities is equally awe-inspiring. Even reading them induces a feeling of exhaustion! He climbed Mont Blanc, Mount Etna and Vesuvius. He toured Norway. In 1858 he toured America and Canada,

33

and the following year went to Russia. And all the time he wrote, talked and sketched. He was one of the great pioneer propagandists, with an extraordinary natural gift for showmanship. Whatever he set his hand to, it was done with the object of persuading others to do likewise—and he was remarkably successful.

In May 1865 his attention focused on the water, but not on boats—on canoes. Recalling the North American canoes he had seen, he designed one, had it built and (of course) named it *Rob Roy*. A preliminary canoe voyage on the river Thames was quickly followed by a whole series, which MacGregor afterwards both described and illustrated in a book entitled *A Thousand Miles in the Rob Roy Canoe on Twenty Lakes and Rivers of Europe*. The new book was a best-seller: it was published in January 1866, and by the middle of May a third edition had made its appearance. Rob Roy gave all profits to the Shipwrecked Mariners' Society and the Lifeboat Institution, which fact was stated on the title page. He gave a lecture before the Institute of Naval Architects. At the Star and Garter Hotel, Richmond-on-Thames, the Canoe Club was founded, and still exists and prospers under the title of the Royal Canoe Club.

It seemed that everything he touched was to flourish, and the 'canoe bug' was to bite thousands. Continental canoe cruising became the rage, especially for young people, undergraduates for whom it represented not only an amusing and adventurous way to see the continent of Europe but also one which they could afford. Small wonder that by the following year, 1867, a new Rob Roy MacGregor book was exciting and welcome news for many. It was a significant year for our purpose here, for it was in 1867 that *The Voyage Alone in the Yawl Rob Roy* appeared.

This, MacGregor's first venture in singlehanded sailing, was conceived partly as an exercise in publicity with philanthropic ends in mind. In 1867 an Exhibition was held in Paris: an exhibition of boats coupled with a Regatta on the Seine. The Emperor Napoleon III himself had ordered the exhibition as an encouragement to young people to acquire a '. . . taste for the exploration of solitary streams and lonely currents . . .' It was all very 'Rob Roy', and indeed it was confidently affirmed that the Emperor had read all about the canoeing ventures. MacGregor decided that he would sail to Paris. The voyage was to be a sort of mission; a large cargo of Protestant tracts would be carried on board with the avowed purpose of helping Rob Roy to bring to that faith as many Roman Catholics as he could, relying on the vigour of his personality and the prestige of his voyage to help him. Subsequently there would also be a book, whose profits would be devoted to training-ships for boys. Few people have been able to combine philanthropy and hedonism so successfully and convincingly as MacGregor. Everything he did he did for the sheer love of it. A voyage such as this gave him ecstatic pleasure, as his writings show. 'I am in extreme enjoyment,' was a frequent expression of his. The boat was a 21ft sailing vessel. In his journal he summarized his voyage as follows: '1867 June 7. Started from Forrest's in my yawl *Rob Roy*, and on September 21 proudly brought her back after three months and a half.' He was extremely pleased with himself and at the end of a letter written in Littlehampton after re-crossing the Channel on the return passage he wrote, 'I feel I have performed a feat and no more be added to it—it is worthy of the Captain of the Canoe Club and I am content.'

It had not been a very arduous voyage, and by comparison with that of Alfred Johnson in *Centennial* was hardly noticeable from the viewpoint of endurance. Rob Roy sailed from Limehouse in the London River to Dover, and from there across the narrow straits to Boulogne in France. Then, coasting along the French coast until he reached Le Havre, he sailed up the Seine to Paris, back again to Le Havre, and from that port across to Littlehampton, whence he made his way back to the Thames. Nothing much to write about perhaps, but John MacGregor not only wrote about the voyage; he lectured tirelessly. His enthusiasm was tremendous and people everywhere found themselves infected. He had had some amusing adventures on his voyage and he made the most of them, but anyone who expected this voyage in the English Channel to prelude a series of larger exploits was to be disappointed! In 1868 MacGregor did make another voyage in *Rob Roy* but it was even less arduous than the first, and in 1871 he sold the yawl to an Australian.

Yet his influence continued to grow. Men of all kinds and creeds bought boats and put to sea. The Reverend William Forwell, a Presbyterian Minister of Broughty

Ferry, read Macgregor's *Voyage Alone*, built a 20ft-long lugger and, taking his fourteen-year-old son with him, set sail for France, and completed a successful cruise. And there were scores like him. John Rob Roy MacGregor may not have made long and difficult sea voyages alone, but he undoubtedly influenced many who were to come later.

In the 1860s, to cruise at all in a small yacht, let alone singlehanded, was an eccentric thing to do. If you went yacht cruising in those days it was in a large well-appointed vessel manned by a professional crew. In his classic story *The Riddle of the Sands* (written in 1903) Erskine Childers so well describes the general atmosphere '. . . the trim gig', to take the passenger out to the vessel, '. . . the obsequious sailors', and the feeling of well-ordered comfort in a craft manned by professionals. The idea of sailing alone in anything large enough to provide accommodation was to invite ridicule in yacht club circles. In this connection it is interesting that Rob Roy considered his boat of 21ft was '. . . the largest that could be well managed in rough weather by one strong man . . .'. When, later, the Victorian stockbroker R. T. McMullen sailed the 42ft-long *Orion* singlehanded, this was considered the height of yacht seamanship. Nowadays much larger boats are sailed singlehanded and nobody thinks it extraordinary at all.

Rob Roy MacGregor has left us some classic paragraphs in his writings. Full of his enthusiasm and knowledge, they are still an inspiration and no bad guide either. A man who wishes to cruise singlehanded should, according to Rob Roy 'have good health and good spirits, and a passion for the sea'. MacGregor was as strong an advocate for doing things alone as was Francis Chichester. A sailor, he would emphasize, had no business to be 'lonely'; he had no time to feel 'lonely'. But it is possible to 'know true loneliness' if you have a companion who is 'soon pumped dry', since now you have 'isolation without freedom all day (and night too) . . .' Rob Roy may not have crossed any oceans, but he was as convinced a 'loner' in his way as Moitessier, Chichester, Gerbault or Colas.

To an American named Bernard Gilfoy, a native of Buffalo, New York, belongs the great honour of being the first to sail across the Pacific singlehanded in a small boat. And 'small' it certainly was, being an 18ft-long dory, 6ft beam and with a draught of 2ft 6in. She was rigged as a cutter, that is with three fore-and-aft working sails, and called *Pacific*. The story of the voyage reads like adventure fiction. This remarkable feat was performed in 1882-3 'for the sake of the pleasure', as Gilfoy himself said, 'he was to get out of it'. He set out on 19 August 1882. Almost six months later he was rescued by a schooner which found him off the Queensland coast. His average speed had been as low as thirty miles in every twenty-four hours. Having provisioned very sensibly for five months (including 150 gallons of fresh water in casks stowed in the fore-part), he set sail from the port of San Francisco, bound on what was termed in a newspaper of the time 'a voyage of pleasure'.

To start with, his passage was uneventful save for the usual irritations of alternating calms and headwinds. But having crossed the equator (on Friday 19 September) he confessed later to a distinct feeling of uneasiness and began to ration food and water. It was his custom to sleep for three or four hours before daylight, since the scorching equatorial sun made sleep virtually impossible. An annoyance which he reported later was that of being disturbed, even in his short hours of rest, by fish bumping into the hull, and flicking it with their tail fins. Especially tiresome were the sharks. Gilfoy reported not one or two but 'dozens', their big dorsal fins criss-crossing in the wake of the boat. To discourage them Gilfoy stabbed at them using his boat hook as a harpoon, and reported that this had had some effect! One of the stratagems which he thought up to discourage the sharks was as follows (in Gilfoy's words): 'Whenever I wanted to take some rest, I slung my shirt over the boat hook and stuck it up in the place where I was accustomed to sit and steer.' It seems this ruse was successful in preventing the sharks from coming too close, since they associated the 'figure' in the stern of the boat with being stabbed at with a boathook.

On 10 November Gilfoy sighted and spoke to the brigantine *Tropic Vance* from Tahiti, which gave him a position with which to check his own. Three weeks or so later came the bad weather: huge seas building up and one so violent that it capsized the boat. Gilfoy managed to get back to the upturned craft and spent an hour righting her. She then capsized a second time, and again Gilfoy managed to right the vessel and bale her out. If for a moment one pictures the conditions of sea in which he did this, it resembles the similar experiences of Alfred Johnson, a feat not far short of miraculous. But as has been

The 3-ton yacht 'Kate', in which Empson Edward Middleton sailed alone round Great Britain. 'Kate', seen here off Torquay, had the same lines as John MacGregor's 'Rob Roy'. Both were typical of the period, the latter part of the 19th century (from the 'Illustrated London News')

proved over and over, a man will do miraculous things to avoid being drowned! Naturally almost all his provisions were lost, likewise both his watch and compass. To add to his troubles the hull of the boat was later rammed by a swordfish and began to leak. When a booby (bird) took perch on his head, he caught it, wrung its neck and ate it then and there.

His condition was truly desperate. He had neither watch nor compass, little water and food, the boat was leaking, even his rudder had been carried away. On Christmas Day he was in the vicinity of Hunter Island, with only twelve pounds of corned meat, two quarts of alcohol and fifteen gallons of water on board. He tried to make for New Caledonia, but both wind and current were against him. By 24 January he had eaten the last of his meat. On the 28th he 'singed' a sea bird over a fire of broken matches and ate it, after which he was reduced to 'sucking barnacles'!

And then by an odd chance of fate the schooner *Alfred Vittery*, bound for Maryborough, sighted Gilfoy on 29

January when he was some 160 miles off Sandy Cape. After a meal, he recovered sufficiently to tell his extraordinary tale, and although he later caught typhoid fever as a result of what he had endured, from even that he was reported on 6 May 1883 as 'having completely recovered'.

The first man to sail the Atlantic singlehanded was, as we have seen, the American Alfred Johnson. *Centennial*, his boat, was 20ft long. Also to an American, Si Lawlor, belongs the record of being the first to sail a really small boat, a mere 15-footer, across the western ocean. He was competing in a race against another 15-footer sailed by fellow-American William Andrews.

In 1878 Andrews had made a crossing from Beverly, Massachusetts, to Mullion in Cornwall, with his brother Asa Walter Andrews as crew. In point of fact, there were a number of Atlantic crossings in the late 1870s in both directions, but all with crew and not singlehanded.

In 1891 William Andrews decided to try to cross alone in his 15ft boat, sloop-rigged, named *Mermaid*. Considerable publicity attended the preliminaries and the venture soon came to the ears of Si Lawlor, who decided to challenge in a boat of similar size. Lawlor and Andrews were well matched. In the 1890s Lawlor had sailed a boat 36ft long (rashly-named *Neversink*) from New York to Le Havre, at the mouth of the river Seine. Si Lawlor's boat was named *Sea Serpent*, and was rigged with a spritsail (like a Thames barge). On 21 June they sailed from Boston. After some weeks at sea both vessels struck a patch of very bad weather and Andrews in *Mermaid* was unlucky enough to be capsized. Although he managed to right the boat and struggle back on board, the effort exhausted him, and being sighted on 22 August by the steamship *Ebruz* he was rescued and brought on board in a state of extreme exhaustion. He had been at sea for sixty-one days.

Si Lawlor aboard *Sea Serpent* was more fortunate, but he too had his moments. Twice the boat heeled right over and was filled with water, and twice Lawlor managed to right her by jumping on her keel. He arrived safely at Coverack, Cornwall, after a passage of forty-five days, making harbour on 5 August. Like Alfred Johnson's crossing, it was a very tough sail and in an even smaller boat.

The year 1894 saw the crossing of the Atlantic (again west to east) by a Finn named Captain Rudolph Frietsch in a boat called *Nina*. If Lawlor's crossing was remarkable partly because of the smallness of his boat, Frietsch also deserves our admiration because *Nina* was a 40ft-long schooner, a tough proposition for a man to manage singlehanded. I have already mentioned that early yachtsmen looked askance at handling large yachts alone, while their modern counterparts appear to make light of it (for example Chay Blyth, Francis Chichester, Jean-Yves Terlain and Alain Colas). Nevertheless, it should be realized that early yachts were designed and built on fishing-boat lines to some extent and cruising yachts had heavy gear—heavy spars, thick rope, big blocks, untractable canvas—by comparison with today's light spars (often of metal), thinner man-made-fibre rope, small light blocks, easily handled light nylon sails etc. Early yachts such as McMullen's *Orion* or Frietsch's *Nina* were very tiring to handle, and a man needed to be extremely fit.

Rudolph Frietsch left New York on 5 August. He made a somewhat slow crossing, experiencing his share of foul weather and arriving off the south-west corner of Ireland on 3 September. On the 5th he appears to have taken on board a man from the crew of the pilot cutter *Geraldine* to assist him into harbour. The sum agreed was £3 (about $12, then), but the fates decreed otherwise; let Lloyds of London finish the story:

London, Thursday, Nov. 7—During a hurricane which prevailed on Tuesday evening and early yesterday morning in the Firth of Clyde the *Nina*, a small schooner-rigged boat, belonging to Captain Frietsch, of Milwaukee, was driven on the rocks in Ettick Bay, at the north end of the island of Bute, and will probably become a total wreck.

Another yacht of about the same size as *Nina* was *Orion*, the 42-footer belonging to R. T. McMullen. Like Rob Roy MacGregor, Richard Turrel McMullen made no great ocean voyages, but similarly exerted a considerable influence on yachting and yachting people both by his example and by his writings. He was born in 1830 and became a member of the London Stock Exchange in 1853; after marriage his wife often sailed with him, although she is seldom mentioned in his logs! He was by all accounts a martinet and a perfectionist, and although he reveals a certain dry humour it is not improbable that in conversation he was a pedant and a bore. Nevertheless he has his undoubted immortality in that he was the first amateur yachtsman to set an example of professional standards of seamanship. He also showed that a largish 42ft vessel can be sailed, navigated, brought into harbour and anchored, all in professional style, by one man; he showed it convincingly, and wrote well about it, and that is the reason for his inclusion here.

Peter Woolass, a modern singlehander, came to this type of sailing partly through difficulty in getting regular crews. McMullen sailed *Orion* singlehanded because his crew were so inefficient and unreliable that he thought he would be better off without them. In the summer of 1877 on 13 July McMullen sailed *Orion* from Greenhithe to Cherbourg. His crew consisted of two men whose names he omits '. . . for the sake of their families, and because I have no desire to be personally vindictive'. In his account of the cruise McMullen is very careful to point out that the men expressed themselves as being 'thoroughly satisfied' both with their accommodation on board and with their pay.

It appears that to start with all went well, and the men asked for £2 (about $8, then) advance to send to their wives. McMullen readily agreed: 'My confidence and respect for them were such that I assented with pleasure.' By 20 July the picture has changed. An entry in the log reads:

July 20—Called the men at 6 am. Had to shift berth by order of harbourmaster, then get ready for leaving the dock at 7.30. When I told George to help get the jib out, he said he would light the fire and clean out the forecastle. Being peremptorily ordered to come, he made an exhibition of himself, and showed that he was master of other than polite language.

This state of affairs worsened, and the climax came when having reached Cherbourg and not wanting to listen to any more 'grumbling', bad language and 'insolence', McMullen decided to dismiss the men. He also decided at the same time to show them that all complaints about his overworking them were unfounded: viz. 'July 28, Saturday—Up to the morning of this day I had been in a state of wretched uncertainty what to do. It vexed me exceedingly that they should go home and report that I

(Overpage) **Victorian small boat pioneer, Richard McMullen, here sailing 'Orion', set by his example and his writings a new high standard for amateur yachtsmen. He made a number of solo passages, some of them in extremely small boats**

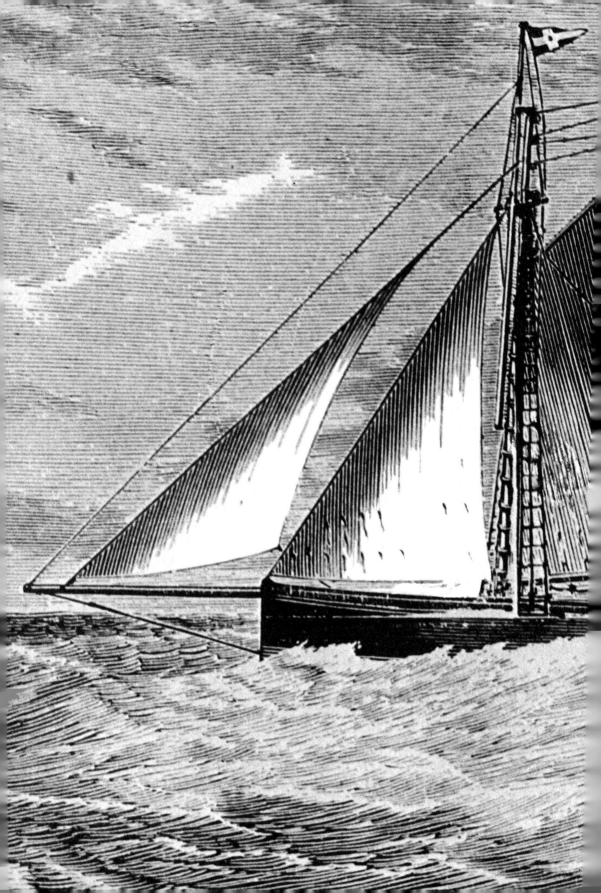

cruelly overworked them—kept them sailing all day, and allowed no proper rest at night.' Suddenly the solution is clear to him. He decides to take 'sole charge' and work back 'singlehanded the way we came'. He thereupon gives them the choice of serving the remaining week or of going back to England immediately on the packet boat. It needs little imagination to guess that they chose the latter!

Having dispensed with his crew McMullen now set about preparing the yacht for sea. He describes the preparation in great detail in his account and one must admit that although everything he did was perfectly correct and good seamanship, he made terrible weather of it. It is as if he is all the time proving to himself that the men had no cause to grumble. He writes in his book, 'I trust this book will be read by some who are interested in labour afloat and ashore; and that something approximating to an estimate of what may reasonably be expected of a man, without complaint of overwork—will be deducted from it.'

I think he achieved his object. Thousands of people have read *Down Channel,* the account of his voyage, and although perhaps nowadays the episode of the lazy crew produces more of a smile than an indignant frown, there remains, after reading McMullen's book, a vivid impression of the pleasure of cruising in small yachts and learning to handle a boat in all weathers. The singlehanded passage from Cherbourg back to Dover was relatively uneventful, and although interesting enough to the student of small boat cruising contains nothing that need be mentioned here. Such a cruise today is relatively commonplace, but in 1877 it certainly was not! Neither were the other cruises McMullen made, sometimes in minute craft like the little 3-ton *Leo.* R. T. McMullen is worthy to be mentioned as a pioneer. He showed what 'could' be done.

What 'could' be done was demonstrated with immortal impact by Captain Joshua Slocum, a professional sailor who singlehanded sailed the sloop *Spray* all round the world. Slocum's place in history is assured, for no matter how many sail round the world, no other man can be the first. Of course he made 'stops' on the way, but he did something which had never been done before. Seamen like McMullen knew that properly handled a well-found small ship can go anywhere. Slocum proved it.

Born in Nova Scotia in 1844, Joshua Slocum was of

seafaring stock, and following tradition grew up to command some of the finest American sailing ships. After a full career 'on the beach', out of work and with jobs very scarce, he was offered 'a ship', which proved to be a hulk propped up in a field. Slocum accepted the vessel and set about rebuilding her. Her name was *Spray*. The job took just over a year and cost him $533.62. His account of the building is delightful, for Slocum wrote excellently, and his book *Sailing Alone Around the World* is a classic.

He was of course a seaman of great experience. The first man to sail a small boat round the world was no amateur yachtsman. He knew the weather and the ocean and all its moods, and how to interpret the hundred little signs that a lifetime of seafaring makes eloquent. His chronometer was an old tin clock. The only time it stopped he cured it by boiling it. He could smell the land when hundreds of miles at sea. If it reads sometimes like a boys' adventure tale, this is Slocum's natural exuberance, and if some of the stories are a little tall who will object? Slocum's natural modesty prompted him to tell us such tales rather than fill the pages of his book with navigational data. The data is there all right, but he makes light of it. The result is a wonderful book, probably the best account of a sail round the world ever written, and that is no insult to others which have followed.

With Joshua Slocum we enter a new phase of single-handed sailing, that of circumnavigating the world. Until then, as we have seen, some remarkable singlehanded voyages had been made, but Slocum was the first to go round the world, a very much bigger undertaking than any previous solo voyage. The *Spray* was 36ft 9in. long. She was very broad, her beam being 15ft. Slocum began his voyage with a passage from Yarmouth in Nova Scotia to Fayal in the Azores, and it took him twenty-two days. It was of course a circumnavigation with 'stops', and indeed we can be grateful for this since it is the slyly humorous descriptions of what occurred at the various 'stops' that make Slocum's book so infinitely readable. What could be more graphic than the following passage from his book, describing the highly social existence he led during his stay in Gibraltar docks?

. . . Later in the day came the hail: 'Spray ahoy! Mrs Bruce would like to come on board and shake hands with

The first to sail alone around the world, Nova Scotiaman, Captain Joshua Slocum, seaman of profound knowledge, whose account of the 46,000-mile voyage is one of the world's classics

the *Spray*. Will it be convenient to-day?' 'Very!' I joyfully shouted. On the following day Sir F. Carrington, at the time Governor of Gibraltar, with other high officers of the garrison, and all the commanders of the battleships, came on board and signed their names in the *Spray*'s log-book. Again there was a hail 'Spray ahoy!' 'Hello!' 'Commander Reynolds' compliments. You are invited on board HMS *Collingwood*, "at home" at 4.30 p.m. Not later than 5.30 p.m.' I had already hinted at the limited amount of my wardrobe, and that I could never succeed as a dude. 'You are expected, sir, in a stovepipe hat and a claw-hammer coat!' 'Then I can't come.' 'Dash it! Come in what you have on; that is what we mean.' 'Aye, aye, sir!' The *Collingwood*'s cheer was good, and had I worn a silk hat as high as the moon I could not have had a better time or been made more at home. An Englishman, even on his great battleship, unbends when the stranger passes his gangway, and when he says 'at home' he means it.

On Monday, 25 August, Slocum eventually sailed from Gibraltar. He had originally intended to sail eastwards through the Mediterranean, but was persuaded to take the course south-east-by-south, across the Atlantic to South America, and so to the Magellan Straits. The reason for this change was that experienced officers at Gibraltar had told him of the very real danger from longshore pirates in the Mediterranean. As it was he was chased by a pirate felucca which fortunately for him was dismasted in a squall. The pirate was gaining on the *Spray* rapidly when this sudden squall struck. Slocum records that he could see the 'thieving crew, some dozen or more of them, struggling to recover their rigging from the sea. Allah blacken their faces!'

Slocum's father was a farmer, but he came of a long line of seafaring folk and Slocum had the sea in his veins. At sixteen he sailed before the mast from St John's to Dublin in a full-rigged ship. He sailed in all sorts of vessels and under different flags, all the time gaining valuable experience, twice rounding Cape Horn in British ships. In 1869 when he was twenty-five years old, he got his first command on a coal-carrying schooner plying between San Francisco and Seattle. In 1870 he was given command of the barque *Washington*, sailing with a general cargo to

Australia and subsequently to Alaska for salmon fishing. In Australia he married, and his new bride was to accompany him on a 6000-mile passage to Alaska.

In northern waters disaster befell *Washington* when she dragged her anchor in a gale and drove ashore without hope of being refloated. Slocum took all the fishing and building gear and materials ashore, and established his fishery in spite of the accident, recruiting Indians to help. He built a 35ft whaler in which they had a good and successful season. Slocum had, in short, shown himself to be courageous and resourceful, and in despite the loss of his ship the owners offered him command of the barquentine *Constitution*.

The year 1873 finds him in command of another great vessel, the barque *Benjamin Aymar*, running between San Francisco, Australia and Shanghai. After this ship was sold at Manila, Slocum met 'a certain Mr Jackson' who had designed a 150-ton steamship. Slocum contracted to build this vessel, which he was perfectly competent to do. He had been in charge of the fishing boats for the Alaskan fishing expedition, having already had considerable experience of boat building. In spite of numerous difficulties he succeeded in building and launching the ship of which he became part-owner.

Another ship-building venture occurred of necessity when at a later stage in his career, having been master and part-owner of the *Northern Light* (said to be the finest American sailing vessel afloat), he bought a small but swift barque, *Aquidneck*. With him was his second wife, Hettie, and his two sons Garfield, five, and Victor, fourteen. Slocum's first wife, Virginia, had tragically died in 1885, at the age of thirty-four. After two years of lonely sailing, carrying freight between Baltimore and Pernambuco, he met a first cousin, Henrietta Elliot, and at the age of forty-two he married the twenty-four-year-old Hettie in Boston. Aboard the new *Aquidneck*, Slocum was to suffer a series of misfortunes culminating in the loss of the ship. Having salvaged as much as possible from the stranded ship, he built a 35ft vessel named *Liberdade*, and having rigged her in Chinese junk fashion sailed himself and his family some 5510 miles in $53\frac{1}{4}$ days from Paranagua to Cape Roman on the coast of Southern Carolina, with various stops on route.

Joshua Slocum thus knew all about both boat building and small ship handling. When out of a job and wondering

Joshua Slocum's *Spray*

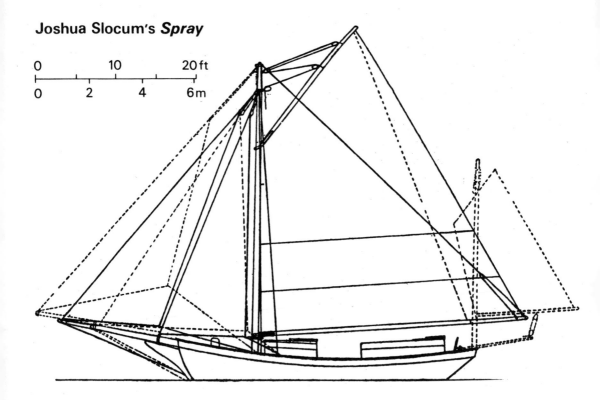

what to do, one day in the winter of 1892 in Boston, a whaling captain acquaintance offered him *Spray*, a ship which wanted 'some repairs'. Slocum himself wrote that 'Next in attractiveness, after sea-faring, came ship-building.' 'From the decks of stout ships, in the worst gales,' he continues, 'I had made calculations as to the size and sort of ship safest for all weather and all seas.' No doubt this wealth of experience contributed greatly to the success of his voyage.

The voyage in the *Liberdade* had been written up by the American press. When he was offered the *Spray* after having been ashore jobless for a year or so, he undoubtedly had the notion of repeating the *Liberdade* venture on a grander, and more profitable scale. He would rebuild the ship, sail her round the world and then write an account of his voyage.

He spent 1893 rebuilding the old *Spray*, and in 1894 he had a season's fishing—not very successful as such—getting to know the boat. In 1895, on 24 April, he sailed from Boston. He was fifty-one years old. Three years later on 27 June 1898 he anchored off Newport. After crossing the Atlantic his remarkable voyage took him to

Gibraltar, south to the Magellan Straits, across the Pacific Ocean to Australia, round the Cape of Good Hope and so once again across the Atlantic ocean to Newport.

Following his return he sailed the *Spray* on pleasure voyages, often to the Caribbean in winter time. When, at the age of sixty-five, he sailed once again on a second long voyage in 1909, he sailed into something of a mystery. He left Bristol, Rhode Island, bound for the Orinoco River. Slocum's son Captain Victor Slocum, observing that the *Spray* would be crossing numerous steamship tracks, believed that his father had been run down by a steamer while below decks either resting, getting a meal, or very probably sleeping. Another view held is that the old ship just broke up in bad weather. Whatever the truth is, after the departure from Bristol neither the *Spray* nor her gallant and gifted master were ever seen again.

Slocum in photographs appears to be a thin, dark man with rather an introspective look about the eyes. His writing would seem to deny this however, for there is no trace of introspection. Like Moitessier today, he had a great love of the sea, but he was also extremely sociable when in harbour, and in this respect more resembles Harry Pidgeon, who in harbour thoroughly enjoyed 'receiving calls from the people on shore,' and the 'merry boys and girls' who 'arrived alongside swimming'. But Pidgeon also wrote when passing through Torres Strait, 'From this point the *Islander* was to follow closely in the track of the *Spray* to the West Indies.' Even today most singlehanders, whether they be builders, sailors or writers, can hardly help following 'the track of the *Spray*' at frequent points.

This first solo circumnavigation was an extraordinary performance. Although he did not sail round the Horn, his passage through the Straits of Magellan was little short of miraculous. Arriving off the eastern entrance of the Straits in February 1896, he met with abnormally bad weather, and in a memorable passage in his book he describes how while asleep some sixth sense woke him: 'I sprang on deck . . . It was now the blackest of nights all around, except away in the South West where rose the old familiar white arch, the terror of Cape Horn, rapidly pushed up by a South West gale. I had only a moment to douse sail and lash all solid when it struck . . . for thirty hours it kept on blowing hard.' On emerging eventually into the Pacific ('I was opening out another world ahead'), Slocum ran slap into a hard gale from the north west. He had to run before it under bare poles, and paid out ropes astern in an attempt to break the huge combers. After four days, he caught a glimpse of a mountain. The Horn? He turned east. But the Horn was still a hundred miles or so to the south, and in fact he entered the Cockburn Channel and so found himself back in the Magellan Straits. But in the entering of that channel was some of the most nightmarish sailing conceivable. 'I saw breakers ahead before long. At this I wore ship and stood offshore, but was immediately startled by the tremendous roaring of breakers again ahead.' He was in a treacherous part of the sea known as the Milky Way, where everywhere the sea breaks white over submerged rocks. As Slocum wrote: 'God knows how my vessel escaped.'

Slocum's vessel, the *Spray*, was by no means an easy craft to sail round the world, being a large, beamy boat with very heavy gear. Yet Slocum's boast that she could, when the helm was lashed, sail herself for hours on end and hold a true course has been proven. His book was eventually published in 1900 by the Century Company, and its author embarked on a sailing tour of America, lecturing and exhibiting the *Spray*. Although he bought a farm near Martha's Vineyard with the profits from this he could never really settle down and his life continued to be that of a water gypsy. In 1906 he got into trouble when the parents of a twelve-year-old girl charged him with rape, but this was later amended to misdemeanour and the charge was not proved. However, Slocum had been held in prison for forty-two days, and in concluding the case the judge remarked that he was 'sorry to be obliged to administer reproof to a man of Slocum's experience and years.' Slocum's resilience soon asserted itself and he continued his curious nomadic, rather sad life. A Pennsylvanian yachtsman who knew Slocum has described him as 'a capable man; and a lonely, unhappy man'.

At the ripe age of sixty-five he began planning another long voyage, to South America, up the Orinoco and right to the source of the Amazon. In pursuit of this Slocum duly sailed from Menemsha bound for Vineyard Haven, Massachusetts. This was to be his last port. When he and the *Spray* left, they ran into a severe gale and were never seen again.

But Slocum had weathered gales before and there are

many conflicting views as to what may have happened to the old boat and her master. It has been admitted by some who remember seeing the *Spray* in her last years, that she had a lot of repairs done; also, she was built from green, unseasoned wood, and this may have told in the end.

It is indeed fortunate that Slocum had a natural flair for expressing himself. Although his publishers had a fair amount of punctuating and editing to do, he had an extraordinary natural gift for prose. The first singlehander to round the world can indeed show us what it was like and will continue to do so as long as there are books to read and men to read them.

In 1899, the year after *Spray* had returned from her round-the-world voyage, a crossing of the Atlantic from Massachusetts to England was made by a remarkable American, Howard Blackburn. His place in any work dealing with singlehanded sailing is assured if only by reason of his almost incredible fortitude. It is difficult to picture a sailor—whose daily business is concerned with ropes and other parts of a ship's running gear—making even a short passage singlehanded if he has no fingers; yet that is what Howard Blackburn did, except that he crossed the Atlantic ocean. He lost his fingers in an accident while serving in a Grand Banks fishing schooner, *Grace L. Fears*. Blackburn and another man called Welch were in one of the schooner's small fishing boats or dories, when a sudden snow storm caught them. It was a storm of peculiar violence, and the two men, unable to see more than a few feet, anchored and waited for the weather to improve. When after nightfall this eventually happened and they were able once more to see the lights of the schooner, they tried to reach her by rowing. But a big sea was still running and being unable to make any headway, they had to anchor again.

It is hard to conjure up on paper the sort of conditions in which Blackburn and Welch found themselves. The irony of it was that their parent ship, the schooner, with food and warmth, was only a mile or so away. One of the worst aspects of their plight was the intense cold. Blackburn had lost his mitts, but gamely kept on bailing and knocking off any ice that formed. So they passed a dreadful day, and another night, and before dawn broke Welch was dead. The following day brought some relief, for the wind and sea went down and Blackburn was able to resume rowing.

It must have been a grim scene with the rower, whose hands were literally frozen round the oars, and his dead companion, propped up in the stern embalmed in a winding sheet of ice. Blackburn's extraordinary tenacity saved him. After another appalling night of bitter cold which only his courage weathered (he could not let himself fall asleep at all, for he knew that if he did he would certainly die), he sighted an island towards which he rowed. Finding an estuary, he rowed up river and was able to land near a small house; it was unoccupied and almost derelict, but, freezing cold as it was, it provided some sort of shelter for the next night even though, once again, Howard Blackburn could not let himself sleep for fear of dying. How many men, having spent three days and three nights at sea in freezing conditions without food and without sleep, would have welcomed death at this point? I suspect a great many! But Blackburn somehow survived the night, and the following day he found a small settlement whose inhabitants gave him the care and primitive medication that saved his life. But nothing could save his hands: he had lost all his fingers, and half of both his thumbs, in addition to all the toes of one of his feet and half of the other foot.

I have quoted this story to give an idea of the extraordinary courage and resilience of the type of seaman typified by Howard Blackburn, a type nurtured by all the great fishing grounds of the world, but perhaps particularly the northern grounds such as the Grand Banks. Blackburn went to sea again after his adventure in another schooner in 1897, making a passage round South America to Alaska, so it is clear that he did not intend the absence of fingers and a few toes to make a longshoreman of him. Returning to his native town of Gloucester, in Massachusetts, a town long famous in the annals of fishing schooners, he had built for his own use a small sloop, 30ft long, and named *Great Western*. He decided to sail from Gloucester, Massachusetts, to Gloucester, England, and set out on June 1899. It was, by comparison, a quiet passage, troubled only by his being unwell for a week or so and by almost being run down by a steamship while still in American waters. Blackburn recorded that he never saw the vessel but that he heard her, and *Great Western* was thrown about violently by the steamer's wash. On 17 August he anchored off Avonmouth, having been sixty

Losing his fingers never stopped Howard Blackburn from going to sea. He twice crossed the Atlantic singlehanded, the second time, in 1901, covering the 2800 miles in thirty-nine days. Here he is seen on his 30ft 'Great Western', 1899 (from the 'Illustrated London News')

days on the crossing, and the next day proceeded to Gloucester to a tremendous reception. But there was very nearly a tragic ending to the story. Having decided to sail up Channel to London, he engaged a crew to help him. All went well until they had rounded the South Foreland, when off the Kentish coast *Great Western* struck the notorious Goodwin Sands. However her end was not to come in this manner, although as far as Blackburn is concerned it came shortly afterwards for he sold her in London, returning to America in a steamer. It almost seems like treachery!

Blackburn's story by no means ended there. No sooner was he back on American soil than he commissioned another boat, smaller than *Great Western,* being 25ft in length and also rigged as a sloop. He named her *Great Republic,* and issued a challenge to any one who would race against him, but no one did, and so once again he sailed singlehanded from Gloucester on 9 June 1901. This crossing was not to be so easy. At one point *Great Republic* was hove to for four days, making no head-way, just weathering out the storm, and he had to battle with another severe gale near the Azores. But on the thirty-eighth day from his departure he sighted land, Cape Espichel south of the Tagus estuary. Another remarkable voyage for a man with no fingers, and especially so since he had only taken thirty-nine days to cover the 2800 miles!

Like her predecessor, *Great Republic* did not return to America on her own bottom but was shipped in a steamer. Blackburn's third singlehanded attempt failed. The boat, a 17ft dory, was the smallest and he named her *America.* He sailed on 7 June 1903 (the year Erskine Childers was busy on the classic sea story *The Riddle of the Sands)*, but he was not to be lucky this time, for he capsized 165 miles east of Cape Sable. Blackburn, in the tradition of Johnson, Andrews and Lawlor, righted the boat and got back aboard to bail. His food had suffered badly from the immersion and his paraffin had gone. Unlike Johnson, however, he decided that enough was enough and returned to harbour.

3

THE ROMANTIC ERA
1900-39

The double-ended, gaff-rigged 'Winnibelle', **in which French artist Marin-Marie sailed the Atlantic, being forty-four days at sea**

WITH THE two voyages of Howard Blackburn we pass from the nineteenth to the twentieth century. In 1903, the year in which Blackburn made his last and unlucky passage, an American German by the name of Ludwig Eisenbraun sailed from Halifax, Nova Scotia, on 28 August, arriving at Gibraltar on 20 November, having called at Funchal (Madeira) en route. His boat, a 19ft sloop, was named *Columbia*. However, it is after the First World War that a significant increase in the number of long-distance singlehanded voyages can be seen. The first passage of note in the 1920s was made by an intriguing character, a French tennis star called Alain Gerbault. With Gerbault we come to one of the early 'between wars' circumnavigators, for although his first passage was a crossing of the Atlantic from east to west in 1924, he continued sailing and eventually completed a circumnavigation of the world in 1929; taking his time about it, and spending much time among the South Pacific Islands, an area which also seems to fascinate his fellow Frenchman, singlehander Bernard Moitessier. Gerbault, like Moitessier, agreed vehemently with Bishop Heber, substituting Polynesia for Ceylon.

Alain Gerbault spent most of his youth in the French north coastal town of Dinard, where to use his own phrase he 'learned to love the sea.' Born in 1893, when the First World War came in 1914 he enlisted in the Flying Corps. While serving, a fellow airman, an American, lent him *The Cruise of the Shark*, a book by Jack London. Gerbault decided that he too was going to sail across oceans one day. In 1921 while visiting a writer friend, Ralph Stock (who wrote *The Cruise of the Dream Ship)*, on board the latter's boat he saw the cutter yacht *Firecrest* lying nearby. *Firecrest* was not a new boat, having been built in 1892, but she represented perfection to Gerbault. It was love at first sight; he bought the yacht and it was in her that he made his great singlehanded passage. She was by no means a small boat, being 39ft overall in length with heavy gear that was bound to tax the strength of the lone yachtsman.

Wisely, Gerbault did not immediately set off across the Atlantic, but having bought the yacht he sailed her to the South of France, being tested on the way by Biscay gales. He cruised about in the Mediterranean for more than a year, usually with a young Englishman as friend and crew, and competed successfully in tennis tournaments on the Riviera, for he was a player of considerable ability.

But all the time a singlehanded passage to America was in his mind. For a year and more he trained strenuously and sailed, fair weather and foul, learning to know his ship in every mood and condition. He was sailing the Atlantic for the fun of it, he said, and to prove that he could do it alone.

Simple enough reasons! But Gerbault was not a 'simple' or straightforward man at all. A thinker and idealist, he has left us two remarkable books—*The Fight of the Firecrest* (about his Atlantic crossing) and *In Quest of the Sun* (the circumnavigation). He enjoyed the hedonistic life on the Riviera, though, and thoroughly relished his role as tennis champion and Riviera playboy. The life may have palled somewhat, however, and the rather masochistic descriptions of discomfort at sea support the idea that the Atlantic voyage was partly in the form of a penance. There is a similarity between Gerbault and Moitessier: both at times seem to wish to escape from the world of men into a dream sea world of ever changing horizons, yet the writings of both ring very true when describing the beauty and the majesty of the sea. Gerbault had in fact made his task harder when he chose a large, elderly boat than usual, especially since *Firecrest*'s sails and running rigging were so worn by the time he came to cross the Atlantic that he spent most of his days making running repairs.

We now come to the actual voyage. The first thing about it was that it created a record. We have seen that the first small boat to cross the Atlantic west to east singlehanded was *Centennial*, sailed by Alfred Johnson. The first to cross from east to west was *Firecrest*, with Alain Gerbault at the helm. He left Gibraltar on 6 June 1924, noting in his log that the 'beautiful' day was a good omen. In contrast to so many ventures begun from British ports in rain and rising winds, Gerbault's log states that having got the vessel sailing on her course he 'lay on deck basking in the sun'. Again in his description of this start of his voyage, the romanticism shines through. He looked forward, he wrote, to 'a sunny run down the Trade Winds to the tropics'. He would find, he adds, 'flying fish and possibly adventure'. It is all most endearing. Pirate schooners and buried treasure were surely just over the horizon. Indeed, just off the

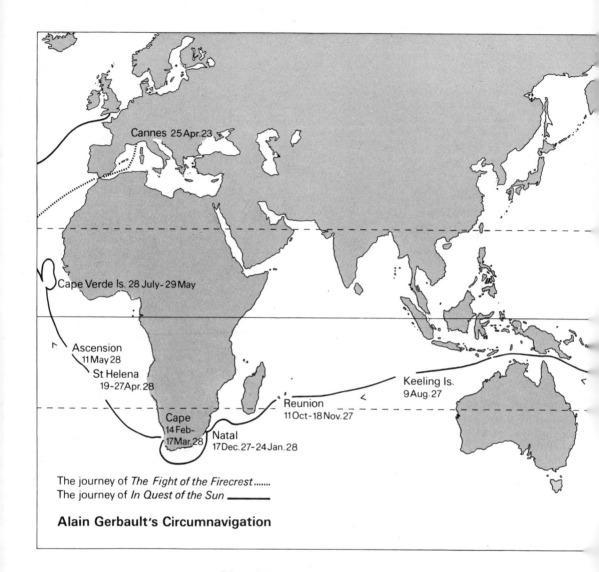

Cannes 25 Apr. 23

Cape Verde Is. 28 July – 29 May

Ascension
11 May 28

St Helena
19 – 27 Apr. 28

Keeling Is.
9 Aug. 27

Reunion
11 Oct – 18 Nov. 27

Cape
14 Feb –
17 Mar. 28

Natal
17 Dec. 27 – 24 Jan. 28

The journey of *The Fight of the Firecrest* ....
The journey of *In Quest of the Sun* ————

Alain Gerbault's Circumnavigation

Moorish coast he did fall in with two large, three-masted schooners and was overjoyed to find that '*Firecrest* could keep up with them.' But the sunbathing on deck was short-lived: off Tangier the wind freshened to gale force, and his jib was blown to pieces, the first of many casualties among his rotten sails. The yacht herself was sound, if of old-fashioned design, having what nowadays would be a very narrow beam (8ft 6in.) for her length and being pro-portionately very deep (7ft). She conformed somewhat to a style of naval architecture disdainfully termed 'plank on edge', not associated particularly with seaworthiness. Nevertheless, the fact was that she carried her lone master around the world, and that speaks for itself. (He did,

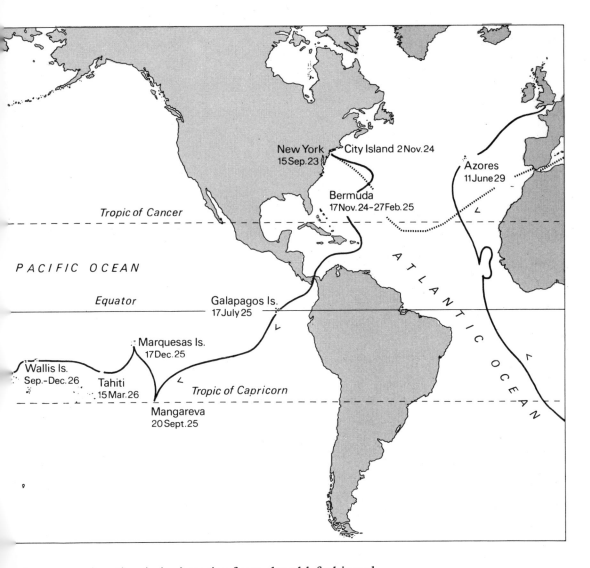

New York 15 Sep. 23

City Island 2 Nov. 24

Azores 11 June 29

Bermuda 17 Nov. 24–27 Feb. 25

Tropic of Cancer

PACIFIC OCEAN

ATLANTIC OCEAN

Equator

Galapagos Is. 17 July 25

Marquesas Is. 17 Dec. 25

Wallis Is. Sep.–Dec. 26

Tahiti 15 Mar. 26

Tropic of Capricorn

Mangareva 20 Sept. 25

however, alter the rig in America from the old-fashioned, four-sided, 'gaff' to the more modern, three-sided, 'Bermudan'.) But sails and running rigging were in poor shape, and in the testing weather that he encountered were to let him down again and again.

If there were faults in his ship, however, they were insignificant compared with Gerbault's enthusiasm for his venture. Whatever sat at the prow or in the hold, confidence was certainly at the helm! He met with a good deal of bad weather on the Atlantic crossing, and it was the best thing that could have happened to him. It tempered the steel of his adventurous spirit, and gave him faith in his ship and true confidence in his ability as a seaman. The gales had come and he had not been found wanting. His subsequent voyage round the world, after changing the yacht's rig in New York, was a leisurely affair taking four and a half years. But when eventually he arrived back at Le Havre in 1929 it was to a tremendous ovation. Gerbault is one of the most interesting of all the—relatively—modern singlehanders. He was a simple person at heart and a man who liked solitude for its own sake; he appreciated the sea and wrote about it without getting submerged in the trough of sentimentality or striking exaggerated attitudes. He was a true singlehander.

If the period 'between the wars' saw an increase in the number of singlehanded ocean wanderers, it undoubtedly saw an increase in the number of worldgirdlers. At noon on 18 November 1921 there sailed from Los Angeles, bound for the Marquesas Islands in the Pacific, a small yacht called *Islander*. At the helm was a man who was not only her skipper and owner, he had built her himself. His name, famous in world-circumnavigation singlehanded history, was Harry Pidgeon.

Born on a farm in Iowa, Pidgeon did not even see the sea until he was eight years old. But while on a ranch in California he acquired, like Rob Roy MacGregor, a taste for canoeing which led to a visit to Alaska, where he and a young farmer built a wooden canoe designed to navigate the Alaska river. His adventure gave him a taste for boating, and he soon built a small boat for use on his Alaskan hunting trips. But all the while an idea was forming. As he put it, he wanted to 'see more distant lands in a vessel of my own'. So far no mention, however, of doing it singlehanded. His dream ship revealed herself to him in the shape of some plans, the design of Captain Thomas Fleming Day, editor of the magazine *Rudder* and a yachtsman of great experience. The plans were for a 'V' bottom or chine construction boat, a method which is easier for the amateur builder. The dimensions of the vessel were 34ft long and 10ft 9in. wide, quite a sizeable boat for home building. The rig was that of a gaff yawl; there was also a 10ft skiff for use as a dinghy/lifeboat, and there was no engine.

Pidgeon laid the keel in 1917. It took him a year and a half to build his boat, and the cost was about $1,000. She was duly launched, and after some preliminary experimental cruises and a course in navigation, Harry Pidgeon and

Islander were ready for the deep blue waters of the ocean.

His first voyage was to Hawaii, and even on this first passage he decided to go singlehanded. Like many another sailor, Pidgeon—fortunately for us—could express himself well on paper and has left an excellent account of his circumnavigation called simply *Around the World Single-handed*. Pidgeon explains his preference for solo sailing as follows: '. . . I like company as well as anyone, but in my wanderings I had already learned to go it alone.' An explanation that leaves a good deal unexplained! In fact he did take a crew for the return passage from Hawaii, a young Californian who had become friendly during Pidgeon's stay on the island and proposed himself as crew. Pidgeon writes that as this young man had had no more experience of sailing boats than washing dishes on a liner there would not appear to any 'danger of his wanting to take charge of the ship'. Already the explanation for Pidgeon's preference for singlehanding is becoming clearer.

When, however, Pidgeon was preparing for his long cruise (he did not at first plan to go all the way round the world), he did consider taking his friend, whose name was Earl Brooks, with him. But after thinking the matter over, and no doubt influenced by the memory of a night of bad weather on the passage from Hawaii, Brooks decided to stay ashore. 'So I went Singlehanded;' wrote Pidgeon, adding that once under way he was glad to be alone. 'It was', he said, 'only the starting that was hard.' (How eloquently simple that is. It says everything. Hemingway could not have bettered it!) So on 18 November 1921, Harry Pidgeon and *Islander* left for Los Angeles.

His intention was to sail to the Marquesas, the Society Islands and Samoa and then return to California, but even at this early stage he admitted that he might go further. Apparently, he decided to go right round the world at Thursday Island, a gravelly strip of land in the reef-strewn Torres Strait. This island is almost unsurpassed for bleakness, but it is a sort of crossroads of the sea from which the mariner can go south to Australia, past the East Indies to the Philippines, or—as Pidgeon chose—to the Cape of Good Hope, the Atlantic, the Panama Canal and so back to California. In fact as we have already noted, he followed quite closely in the wake of Captain Joshua Slocum's *Spray*, which had passed through Torres Strait in June 1897. Harry Pidgeon's book is infectiously high-

spirited: he loved every minute of his lonely voyage, even finding a night collision with a liner off the South American coast 'the most thrilling five minutes of my voyage'.

Islander finally returned to Los Angeles harbour on 31 October 1925, the circumnavigation having taken three years, eleven months and thirteen days. Pidgeon stated that his voyage was not made 'for the joy of sailing alone', but because it was his own way of seeing something of the world, and he adds that the days he spent were the freest and happiest of his life. Indeed, if proof were needed of the truth of those words, Pidgeon made another circumnavigation in *Islander* in the 1930s. He sailed from New London, USA, back to New London via Panama and New Guinea, but whereas his first round-the-world voyage had taken just under four years, the second time he took five, starting in 1932 and completing the circumnavigation in 1937. Harry Pidgeon can truly be called one of the most experienced long distance singlehanders of all time.

In the late 1920s four unusual men held the singlehander stage: two Germans, Franz Romer and Paul Muller; Thomas Drake, English-born but American by adoption; and Edward Miles, an American. In 1926 Captain Thomas Drake sailed across the Atlantic from Charleston in South Carolina in a yacht called *Pilgrim*. He had much in common with Joshua Slocum in that he was a Master Mariner who liked singlehanded sailing in small boats, which he built himself; also like Slocum, he took to singlehanded sailing relatively late in his life. Although not among the circumnavigators, he made a large number of voyages, and long before he sailed *Pilgrim* across the Atlantic he had spent many years sailing around the world in square-rigged ships. His first small boat which he built for himself was a schooner which he named *Sir Francis*. In this vessel he cruised extensively in the Pacific and the Caribbean, but eventually lost *Sir Francis* near Port Angel, Oaxaca, when she was forced ashore. However, Drake was soon at sea again in another self-built boat.

His most famous vessel was undoubtedly *Pilgrim*, the 35-footer in which he crossed the Atlantic, arriving off the Cornish coast after a relatively uneventful passage except for a severe gale at the very end. The crossing took him fifty-two days. He was sixty-six when *Pilgrim* was wrecked off the Dutch coast in 1929; he was sailing from Scandinavia to France, having sailed some 30,000 miles in

(Left) **A dream begins to come true—Harry Pidgeon's** 'Islander', **which he built himself and in which he circumnavigated the world, begins to take shape**

(Below left) **American singlehander Harry Pidgeon launching** 'Islander'. **Her keel was laid in 1917 and it took Pidgeon one and a half years to build her. The three-year voyage ended in October 1925. Pidgeon made another circumnavigation 1932-7** four years cruising. He returned to America where he at once built another boat, *Progress*, a 37-footer in which he rode out a full gale in the Pacific. *Progress* suffered considerable damage as did her owner, who broke his right arm. Like Danny Kaye, as Walter Mitty, he carried on, stating later that he had 'managed all right' with his remaining good arm and hand. When his arm had healed, he set off again in a repaired and refitted *Progress* on a long voyage to the South Seas. He was by now seventy-three years old, but the luck which had been with him for so long now deserted him and he disappeared, presumably drowned. A tragic end to a great sailor and a seaman of vast experience, which is once again reminiscent of Slocum.

Next chronologically comes the first of the two Germans, Franz Romer, who in 1928 made an east-to-west crossing of the Atlantic in a canvas-covered canoe, *Deutscher Sport*, which was 21ft 6in. long by 3ft of beam. Romer left Lisbon on 28 March 1928, arrived without mishap at Las Palmas, Canary Islands on 10 May and left again on 2 June. He reached St Thomas in the West Indies on 30 July, having sailed 3485 miles and spent fifty-eight days at sea. 21ft 6in. may not seem too bad after *Centennial*'s 20ft, or *Sea Serpent*'s 15ft, but even little *Sea Serpent* had 5ft of beam. The meagre 3ft of *Deutscher Sport* makes those three and a half thousand miles seem a terribly long way! Romer's wanderings in this narrow and constricted vessel came to a tragic end, for having left St Thomas again on 12 September he was lost at sea in a hurricane.

The round-the-world voyage of American singlehander Edward Miles also began in 1928. He left New York on 28 August 1928, in a 35ft vessel named *Sturdy*, crossed the Atlantic without incident and entered the Mediterranean by the Straits of Gibraltar. However, having passed through the Suez Canal his ship caught fire in the Red Sea and became a total loss. Undaunted, Miles had a second vessel built, named her *Sturdy II* and a year later continued the circumnavigation, returning to New York in August 1932.

The second German, Paul Muller, had another very small boat; lugger-rigged, she measured only 18ft by 6ft. Named *Aga*, her voyage began in July 1928 in Hamburg, and was to end in Miami on 1 June a year later. Muller's port of departure for the Atlantic crossing was Cape Juby in Spanish West Africa. It was a remarkable voyage.

To start with, Muller was broke. Furthermore, he knew absolutely nothing about handling boats His vessel, a seventeen-year-old fishing boat, bore written across her lugsail the optimistic legend 'from Hamburg to America'. From the outset his voyage was hazardous. He left in a hurry (wanted by the police for fighting), ran aground off Cuxhaven, was rescued by a fisherman and—like Davies in *The Riddle of the Sands*—towed to the safety of one of the Friesland harbours. There the kindly Dutch looked after him and no doubt added to his pathetically minute stores and equipment. One can hardly call it equipment; seldom has a potential Atlantic crosser been so ill-equipped! He ran into further trouble in Ostend; Germans were not popular there in 1928, moreover he had no passport. As at Hamburg, he left quietly and in a hurry.

In the Channel bad weather continued to pursue him. Hopping from port to port along the north French coast, he dodged the police and the customs and from time to time received help and monetary assistance, once from a fellow German in Le Havre and again in Cherbourg from an Englishman. One can picture Paul Muller; no doubt he had his share of raffish charm.

In the Channel Islands his boat was refitted and his stores replenished; this entirely due to the good-heartedness of the Islanders. So he continued, eventually making Brest and then south across the Bay of Biscay to Biarritz. With the lugsail rig of Muller's boat there was no headsail in front of the mast. It is a very inefficient rig, a poor performer except plain 'down wind', all of which makes Muller's achievement the more remarkable. He was again fortunate in north Spain and in Portugal, collecting or 'conning' stores and gear, and was well received and entertained by the German consul in Oporto who, confined to his routine consular existence in a foreign land, may well have found something refreshing in the free-roaming adventurer from his own country.

His luck still holding, Muller continued his voyage with a sail direct to Rabat in Morocco where, back on French soil, he had a warm reception, even being threatened with imprisonment for vagrancy! Leaving Rabat in a hurry, he sailed to Mogador, making light of a full gale on the way.

After many delays he reached Cape Juby, from which desolate spot he was glad to sail on 14 February, bound for the Canary Islands. From Las Palmas he then made the long crossing, landing at the Bahama Islands in a state of extreme exhaustion caused mainly by lack of food. He stayed in the Bahamas long enough to recover and then sailed to Cuba, Havana, where he was given a hero's welcome!

From Havana he continued to Miami, arriving on 1 June, but after a stay of only a few days he sailed for New York. He fell asleep at the tiller and ran *Aga* ashore on the northern part of the Florida peninsula. The boat was damaged, but not irreparably, and after having it repaired the indomitable Muller resumed his passage north. The repairs were less sound than they might have been, for *Aga* was making water, and with the arrival of bad weather the leaks grew serious, so Muller ran her ashore and beached her, this time deliberately. It is recounted that he set fire to the little ship, having saturated the wreck with paraffin; seemingly a strange thing to do, but perhaps those who have read James Weston Martyr's classic *The Southseaman* will understand.

This tale ends curiously. After some difficulties over his identification, the plausible Muller sufficiently ingratiated himself with the authorities to be given a new boat, *Aga II*. At the corporation's expense he lived in a hotel for two months, during which time he not only fitted out *Aga II* but married a German girl with whom he set off again. This voyage was not to prosper, for he was wrecked off Cape Hatteras and *Aga II* was a total loss. Even this was by no means the end of Muller's adventure, but it is the end of his activities as a singlehander, and it is really with the wreck of his beloved *Aga* the first, blazing on the Florida shore after having carried him well over six thousand miles since Hamburg, that we must leave him.

With the 1930s we now come to a notable increase in the number of long-distance singlehanded passages. A remarkable voyage from Australia to Los Angeles in the USA was made singlehanded aboard a 19ft skiff, by Fred Rebell, a building contractor of Sydney, Australia in 1931-3, thus establishing a record as being the first to cross the Pacific Ocean from west to east. Rebell was born in Windau, Latvia, when it was part of Tsarist Russia, but later went to Australia. While he was there, Latvia became a republic, but since Rebell had not taken Australian citizenship he was a man without a country.

This was a good example of the power of determination. Rebell, whom the press labelled the 'height of folly navigator', in fact taught himself navigation in three weeks in a library at Sydney. He took with him two dollar watches as his chronometers, and even built his own sextant for taking bearings of the sun, moon and stars.

His boat, a clinker-built skiff with a large bowsprit and sloop rig, he named *Elaine* after an Australian girl. He rigged a canvas canopy over most of the skiff's open cockpit. She was very narrow, with a beam of 5ft, and her freeboard was as little as twenty inches. What a craft in which to sail across the Pacific! He coated his water tanks with bitumastic, and when filled he estimated that they would last him four months. With barley, oats, rye and other cereal, he had, he reckoned, six months' provisions. *Elaine* and her skipper sailed in December 1931, cruising through the southern Pacific islands. On reaching Honolulu he managed to get a sixty-day distressed seaman's permit, but from there to Los Angeles took him sixty-six days. He was arrested as he stepped ashore and held in the immigration station since his permit had expired and he was a 'stateless' man! He was rescued from his plight by the author William Slavens McNutt, but a tragic end to his great voyage came when little *Elaine*, which had borne him so well over many thousands of miles of the Pacific, was wrecked in a storm inside Los Angeles breakwater.

Among those who, for example, crossed the Atlantic in those years were a number of French singlehanders. In 1933 a French artist, Marin-Marie, made the crossing from Douarnenez to New York, calling at Funchal, Madeira, en route. His boat was named *Winnibelle*, and was forty-four days at sea. Marin-Marie brought off an unusual 'double', in that in 1936 he motored from New York to Ile Chausey in France, non-stop, in the 45ft motor cruiser *Arielle* driven by what nowadays seems the extremely modest power of a 15h.p. Badaouin diesel engine. The Atlantic was first 'motored' as long ago as 1902, in the 38ft life-boat *Abiel Abbott Low*. The editor of *Rudder,* always prepared to do anything, motored the crossing in a 35-footer in 1912, and in 1950 the passage was made in a 15ft amphibious jeep, appropriately named *Half Safe,* driven by the Australian F. B. Carlin. But unlike Marin-Marie, these had at least one crew.

In 1936 a gallant Frenchman named Louis Bernicot

made a solo circumnavigation when fifty-two years old. In the 38ft sloop *Anahita* he sailed from Carantec round the world via the Straits of Magellan and the Cape of Good Hope, returning to Verdon after one year, nine months and twenty-two days.

Yet another Frenchman (or more strictly a French-American) who crossed the Atlantic solo (from New York to Spain) was Jean Gau. His boat, the 40ft schooner *Onda*, was wrecked near Cadiz on the Spanish coast. Jean Gau made it successfully in 1947, sailing a 29ft ketch *Atom* from New York to Marseilles, with one stop at the Azores.

A man who certainly deserves mention here is Francis Edward Clark. He bought his boat *Girl Kathleen* when he was fifty-seven years of age; he was moreover one of the few men who have crossed the Atlantic both ways, east to west and west to east singlehanded. In *Girl Kathleen* Clark left Portsmouth on 23 August 1938. He had an uneventful passage until he reached the Bahamas, where he en-

(Above) **Returning to Le Havre after a six-year voyage round the world, Alain Gerbault is greeted by friends who have rushed to meet him as he lands his beloved** 'Firecrest'

(Left) **The trim yawl** 'Stoertebaker III', **in which the German yachtsman Ludwig Schlimbach crossed from Lisbon to New York in 1937**

countered a hurricane which in the account of his voyage he described as the 'worst hurricane I have known'. Clark, British by birth, spent much time in America. He had a varied experience in many waters, including the Great Lakes and 'Rum Row', that elusive smugglers' anchorage which has nevertheless, on one occasion at least, been described as 'fifteen mile east sou' east o' Montauk point'. (Montauk Point is at the eastern end of Long Island.)

The hurricane lasted six days. Food ran out and so did fresh water, and when he managed to reach Savannah, South Carolina, on 10 November, Clark was in an utterly exhausted condition. Rescued by coastguards, he was put in prison, for he had not changed the registration of his boat in Portsmouth and could produce no papers to prove ownership. However, in due course friends in New York came to his rescue.

Clark's account of his voyage tells how he ran foul of Savannah dope smugglers who acquired his boat, and how by devious means he managed to steal it back again and run for New York. There is always something faintly incredible about Clark. What is quite certain is that on 15 June 1939 he sailed back to England, arriving at Newlyn in Cornwall on 16 July, after taking thirty-three days from New York, thus completing the two-way trip. In August of 1939 he sailed again from Portsmouth, arriving in the Azores after a testing passage in foul weather. The Second World War began in September, and although nothing is known for certain, it is believed that Clark was taken prisoner by the Germans at or near Walvis Bay on the coast of Africa.

It is not my purpose in this book to produce a definitive history of singlehanded sailing sailors, and this I have already stated. We are looking, rather, at a number of typical solo-sailors, but we are also considering the whys and the wherefores and the problems—and delights—involved. It seems right to reiterate this here, since in the 1930s and since the Second World War, there has been a considerable increase in the number of singlehanders and to include them all would most assuredly defeat my purpose.

Even in the 1930s yachtsmen of all nationalities, types and ages were trying their hand at long-distance lone voyaging. In 1932 a Norwegian, Alfon Hansen, sailed the Pilot cutter *Mary Jane* from Norway to Mississippi. The following year Commander R. D. Graham, RN, sailed singlehanded from Newfoundland to Bermuda in the gaff cutter *Emanuel*. In 1937 the German Ludwig Schlimbach sailed the yawl *Stoertebaker III* from Lisbon to New York, and in the following year another German, Heinrich Garbers, sailed from Spain in *Brezza III*, a voyage which had begun originally at Hamburg, and which took fifty days to reach New York while the events of the 'Munich crisis' were reaching a crescendo.

4

THE ESCAPIST ERA
The 1940s and 1950s

THE SECOND World War turned Australian John Caldwell into a singlehander. He sailed 9000 miles across the Pacific to his young bride in Australia because there was no other way to get to her. In many respects as a singlehander he is unique, and his graphic description of being in the centre of a hurricane in a small yacht has never been bettered. Secondly, Caldwell is probably one of the most naive singlehanded sailors ever to have grasped a tiller. Not only did he not know how to navigate; he did not know how to sail, and in fact he had only once in his life been in a small boat! His book *Desperate Voyage* is marvellous reading: a straightforward account of how a complete tyro managed to learn to navigate and handle a boat, while at sea; of how he weathered a hurricane, but was dismasted and then sailed for thirty-six days under makeshift rig, hungry and short of water, and of how he eventually managed to run his yacht *Pagan* on a coral reef off the island of Tuvutha in the Fiji Island group. It is a book well worth reading, for he reports exactly what happened to him in complete honesty. This is why his account of being in a hurricane in a small yacht is so valuable as well as fascinating.

With John Caldwell we come to a widening of our scope. To recapitulate: back in the 1890s we find that the singlehanders are mostly Americans: Johnson, Lawlor, Andrews, Slocum and Blackburn for example. After the First World War the activity becomes more international: Gerbault, Jean Gau, and Marin-Marie were French; Pidgeon and Drake, American; Romer, Muller, Eisenbraun, Schlimbach and Garbers, German; Graham, Rees and Clark, British; Alfon Hansen, Norwegian; Fred Rebell, an expatriate Latvian; and so one could continue, but the international aspect is now obvious. After the Second World War this aspect increases, but with two significant changes; there are far more very long passages, circumnavigations, and long-distance singlehanded racing really gets going. Other new factors are the appearance of some formidable lady singlehanders; the perfection of self-steering devices which, with great advances in radio communications, have revolutionized singlehanded sailing, the appearance on the scene (in significant form) of the sponsor, and with this increased activity the controversial subject of expensive rescue service operations.

(Previous pages) **Naval architect Edward C. Allcard on the fo'c'sle of the yawl 'Temptress', a vessel some 40 years old at the time (1949). He made an 81-day crossing of the Atlantic singlehanded**

In our brief examination of these post-Second World War singlehanders, we cannot do better than start with John Guzzwell, who not only sailed a very small boat indeed (18ft 6in. on the waterline) round the world but built the boat as well.

John Guzzwell inherited his love of the sea from his father, who came from the English fishing town of Grimsby, and from his grandfather whose fleet of red-sailed fishing smacks sailed from the same port. He was born in England but grew up in Jersey, one of the Channel Islands, another place where boats are a familiar sight. His father had two yachts, the first built on trawler lines called *Our Boy*, and her successor, an 18ft cutter called *Try Me*. Young John grew up with yachts.

With the outbreak of war in 1939 and the initial German successes, the family tried three times to escape to England in *Try Me*, but bad weather prevented them even though it was only some eighty miles. Then the Germans arrived, occupied Jersey and put an end to their chances of escape. John and his family were not allowed to remain on the island, but together with a number of other families were sent to an internment camp in Germany. During this time John said that although his education may have suffered as a result, at least his father was able to teach him navigation. At the end of the war, the family returned to Jersey, but being quite unable to pick up the thread of their former life, emigrated to South Africa, the homeland of Mrs Guzzwell. But prison life had wrecked John's father's health, and he died in 1948. After two years in South Africa John became restless, and came north to have a look round and visit England and Jersey. Even at this relatively early stage he had decided that the one thing he wanted to do more than anything else was to 'make a long voyage alone'. He had some skill as a joiner and decided he could build his own boat. Remembering the stories his father used to tell him of the logging camps and timbered mountains of British Columbia, John came to a decision: he would emigrate to Canada and build his boat in Victoria, British Columbia.

John Guzzwell arrived in Victoria in March 1953. He rented a room, got himself a job and soon was earning enough to think about building his boat. He seems to have possessed not only his fair share of self-confidence, but an unusual certainty of what he wanted to do. He wrote to a British designer, Jack Laurent Giles, who had produced

John Caldwell's *Pagan*

Overall length 29 ft
Waterline length 25 ft
Beam 9 ft
Bowsprit 8 ft
Mast 33 ft
Deckhouse length 9 ft
Deckhouse height 2 ft
Forward freeboard 30 in.
Aft freeboard 21 in.

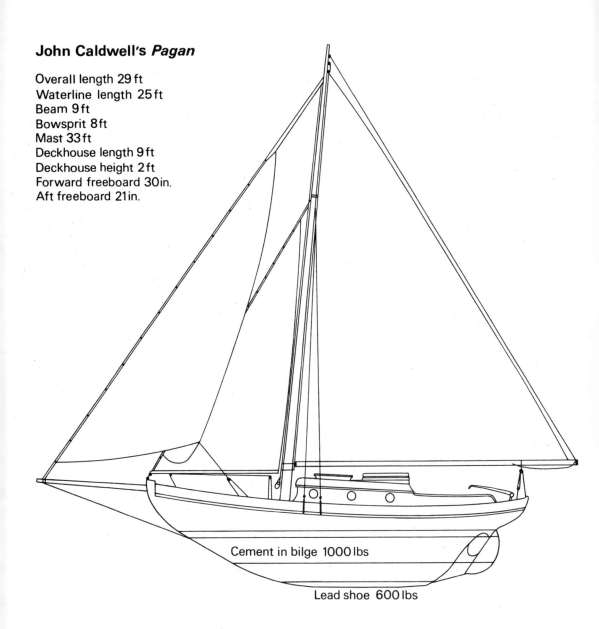

Cement in bilge 1000 lbs

Lead shoe 600 lbs

Below decks plan of *Pagan*

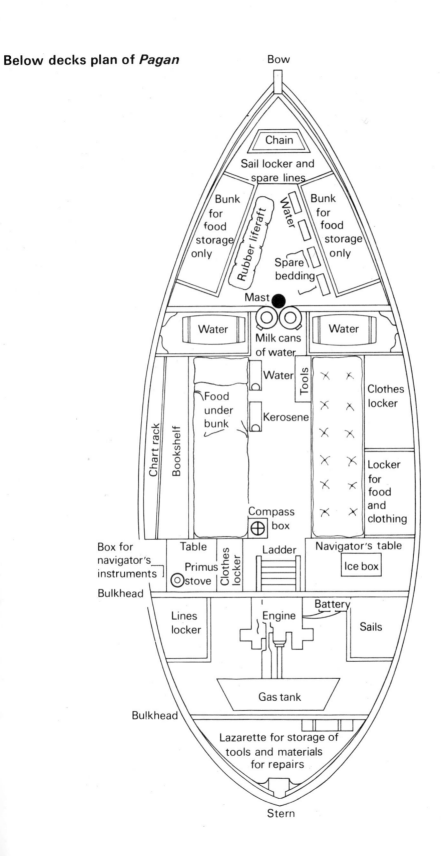

Bow

Chain

Sail locker and spare lines

Bunk for food storage only

Water

Rubber liferaft

Bunk for food storage only

Spare bedding

Mast

Water

Milk cans of water

Water

Water

Tools

Clothes locker

Food under bunk

Kerosene

Chart rack

Bookshelf

Locker for food and clothing

Compass box

Box for navigator's instruments

Table

Clothes locker

Ladder

Navigator's table

Primus

Ostove

Ice box

Bulkhead

Lines locker

Engine

Battery

Sails

Gas tank

Bulkhead

Lazarette for storage of tools and materials for repairs

Stern

the plans of a number of successful small ocean-going yachts. On receiving the design which Giles sent he was delighted, for the small 18ft 8in. waterline, 6ft 6in. beam, was what he wanted in every respect. He found himself an old storeroom at the back of a fish and chips shop, bought a book on boatbuilding and set to work.

In his book *Trekka Round the World* Guzzwell includes an excellent description of how he built his little boat, and how eventually she was launched and named *Trekka* from the South African word *Trek* meaning 'to make a journey'. Like the modesty with which Guzzwell dismissed a difficult building job the name was something of an understatement! For building *Trekka* was neither quick nor easy. She was round-bilged, not 'chine' like Pidgeon's *Islander,* and there were more than 3000 fastenings to rivet over. The new boat was ready for her launching towards the end of August 1954. Guzzwell spent the spring of 1955 getting to know his craft, and then one Saturday—10 September—he was ready to leave.

He sailed south from Victoria to San Francisco. Here he met the Smeetons, Miles and Beryl and their young daughter Clio, cruising in a ketch called *Tzu Hang,* and they became friendly. The result was a cruise in company to Hawaii.

In several ways Guzzwell's and Harry Pidgeon's first voyages are similar. Both built their own boats. Both made a preliminary cruise to Hawaii. While in Hawaii, Guzzwell and the Smeetons decided to continue cruising in company to the southern Pacific. This was an ideal arrangement, and it will already be clear that Guzzwell, while preferring to sail alone, nevertheless found sailing in company with another yacht very congenial, and in this he is unlike a number of his fellow singlehanders, who seemed to prefer being 'lone wolves' all the time except possibly in harbour. Most of them believed firmly in the old saying that 'the sea is for sailing upon and that harbours rot good ships and men'; but not all of them; some, like Joshua Slocum, could combine lone sailing with a thoroughly social life ashore.

John Guzzwell's 18ft 6in (waterline) 'Trekka'. Built by himself, she made a circumnavigation in the 1950s, a voyage full of incident superbly recounted in Guzzwell's excellent book

Guzzwell had arrived in the Hawaiian Islands on 2 September. His course southward took him via Fanning Island (a small coral island, about 1100 miles south of Honolulu) and Samoa. All the time he sailed a similar course to *Tzu Hang,* though by no means always in company. From Samoa he sailed south-west to Vavau, in

the northern Tongan group, and after passing through alternate periods of fierce squalls and calms arrived in Russell in New Zealand on 30 May 1956.

His singlehanded voyage was now to have an interruption of two years. In December of 1956 he sailed aboard *Tzu Hang* with the Smeetons, who had asked him to ship as crew for a passage round Cape Horn. This voyage lasted from 26 December 1956 to 21 March 1957. It was a voyage of disaster, *Tzu Hang* being toppled completely stern over bow by a freak wave which dismasted her and stripped her decks bare. Luckily she floated, although full of water. How the Smeetons and Guzzwell got her to the South American coast is, as already mentioned, the subject of Miles Smeeton's book.

After this interlude Guzzwell, leaving the Smeetons in Chile having helped them with the biggest repair jobs, flew to South Africa to see his mother in Natal. He found her preparing to leave and return to the Channel Islands, so accompanied her to Jersey and helped her settle in, eventually taking a ship in London bound for Sydney, there being no available liner to New Zealand. When he eventually stepped on board *Trekka* in Auckland he had been away for sixteen months, but with the experiences aboard *Tzu Hang* these were by no means wasted.

Guzzwell was overjoyed to be back with his boat. Before continuing his voyage he had to fit her out, which included giving her wooden hull a sheath of fibre-glass. He was given encouragement and assistance by many friends, including particularly a couple called Arlidge. All through Guzzwell's voyage, one of the things that stand out is his capacity for making friends along the way. Sailing alone across the Tasman Sea, up through the Great Barrier Reef, through Torres Strait and the Arafura Sea to the Cocos Islands, we soon find him, at Middle Island, falling cheerfully in with an Englishman, Norman Young, sailing a converted Falmouth Quay punt with the help of three others. These four, in their old boat *Diana*, were bound for South Africa; and so the two boats sailed in company arriving at Thursday Island in the Torres Strait on 4 September 1958. Guzzwell spent the autumn and early winter crossing the Indian Ocean and arrived at Durban on 2 December. While there he met a young South African who had recently returned from Canada. He told Guzzwell of a man he had met while in Canada who was building a boat, and it turned out that Guzzwell was that man! Either the South African's memory was poor or Guzzwell had altered somewhat in appearance. The latter is quite possible. Sailing of this kind tends to harden one, removing surplus fat and fining down the features. It can also change one in other ways as we shall see later.

Leaving Durban on 15 January 1959, John Guzzwell soon found himself hove-to in a gale during which time he made over fifty miles under current alone. He arrived off Cape Town without mishap and the rest of his cruise, though full of lively incident, presented no really serious problems. It had been his intention to complete his circumnavigation by sailing back to Hawaii. From Cape Town he sailed north west to the Panama Canal. He did not intend to go 'round the Horn' and in this connection it is interesting to note that Guzzwell's circumnavigation, had he rounded the Horn on the way back to the Pacific, would have been like Chay Blyth's 'the wrong way round'; that is to say, against the westerly trend. But a look at the maps and charts which illustrate Chapter 6 will show that Guzzwell, by keeping well north of the Roaring Forties, was able to make use of other favourable currents. Joshua Slocum had taken the same course. Slocum did go down to Cape Horn, but he sailed through the Straits of Magellan and then almost due north to Juan Fernandez Island and away from the Roaring Forties. The use which the singlehander may make of the wind systems and currents is discussed more fully in Chapter 6.

Coming at last to the final stage of his great voyage, John Guzzwell left Balboa, Panama, on the afternoon of 21 May. He arrived in the Hawaiian Islands sixty-two days later, a long enough solo passage in itself and containing a succession of severe gales. When he sighted the peak of Mauna Kea sixty miles away, he opened his last can of Australian Christmas pudding to celebrate. That modest celebration—no champagne, no histrionics—is typical of the man. And when he finally arrives at the Ala Wai Yacht Basin he records this tremendous fact simply by writing 'I . . . moored against the gas dock, where I waited for the authorities to clear me. It had been a very long passage.'

We now come to consider a new factor in singlehanded sailing, the addition of the racing element, and a significant factor it is. But before we do so let us enumerate—albeit briefly—a number of significant singlehanded passages made since the outbreak of the Second World War and not already mentioned. The first must be that of Vito Dumas, in 1942. Dumas was born in the Argentine in 1900. Author of the book *Alone Through the Roaring Forties,* he could be said to be a singlehander of enormous experience since not only did he make many long solo passages, but in 1942-3 rounded the world singlehanded. In the 30ft ketch *Lehg II,* Dumas sailed from Montevideo, to make the first singlehanded circumnavigation from west to east by the southern route. Dumas was a really remarkable ocean voyager, sailing alone for a quarter of a century all over the world. His circumnavigation in 1942-3 brought every kind of tribulation too, including an infection of his right arm. During a gale he continually had to inject himself in an effort to save the arm, but after a week during which the infection grew perceptibly worse, he thought seriously of amputation. However, this proved to be unnecessary, the wound healing itself, a remarkable instance of the ability of the human body to do just that.

In 1948 a circumnavigation from New York to New York was made in a 22-year-old Colin Archer double-ended Typical Norwegian Lifeboat-type cutter called *Stornoway.* The singlehander, an American by the name of Alfred Petersen, left in June, sailed via Panama, Torres Strait and the Suez Canal, and arrived at his home port in August 1952.

Two remarkable French singlehanders were Jacques-Yves le Toumelin and Alain Bombard. Le Toumelin's boat *Kurun* was 33ft long. He sailed from Le Croisic in France on 9 September 1949, crossed the Atlantic to the Panama Canal and went on to make a circumnavigation lasting two years, nine months and two weeks. As far as Tahiti Le Toumelin had a crew, but from then on it was a solo effort. A similar circumnavigation, 'semi-singlehanded', was made by American W. T. Murnham in 1947-52 in the yawl *Seven Seas,* since Murnham had his wife as crew for a part of the time.

The other Frenchman, Dr Alain Bombard, made an Atlantic crossing for primarily medico-scientific reasons. He wished to research the length of time that a man or woman, adrift for whatever reason in a small boat or raft, without either food or water, could live. Bombard's contention was that provided the shipwrecked man could catch fish and plankton and had certain implements to

'Kurun' **off Le Croisic. In
this double-ended gaff
cutter Le Toumelin left
Le Croisic on
9 September 1949. He
made a
circumnavigation, with
a crew as far as Tahiti,
singlehanded there on**

assist him, he could survive indefinitely. It is interesting in this connection to note how long the Robertson family were recently able to do just this in the South Pacific after their yacht had been sunk in an attack by killer whales. Dougal Robertson's book *Survive the Savage Sea* describes vividly the stoical and sensible way in which the family did literally 'survive' the sea and appalling dehydration until rescued.

Bombard maintained that man can live on sea water for a period of up to about two weeks, provided it is taken in extremely small quantities. He set great store by plankton, the eating of which he maintained provided protection against scurvy.

However, the oddest thing about Bombard was the vessel in which he made his crossing. It was a life-raft of pneumatic air-containers, with leeboards or side keels like a Dutch fishing boat, and a small, stumpy mast supporting a diminutive sail. Bombard was, of course, emulating '*raft*' conditions. His successful crossing took him singlehanded from Casablanca (leaving on 25 August 1952) to Bridgetown in Barbados. The passage took seventy-seven days, and he called at Las Palmas on the way. The distance sailed was 3150 miles, a long way by any account, but the remarkable fact was that Bombard deliberately took *neither food nor fresh water* with him. His voyage was to give tremendous hope to all who might have the misfortune to find themselves shipwrecked and alone at sea in a tiny boat without provisions. The passage non-stop from Las Palmas to the West Indies took sixty-four days; to survive that without food or water was indeed a remarkable achievement.

Other notable Atlantic crossings of this period included that of the American Clyde Deal who sailed from Gibraltar to New York in the 33ft ketch-rigged *Ram*. Around 30ft seems to be a very popular length and rightly so, for a boat this long constitutes the happy medium in that she is neither too big nor her gear too heavy for one man, while at the same time providing reasonable comfort both in space below and in her motion at sea. Smaller boats, of say 20ft or so on the water-line, tend as an old sailor put it long ago 'to dip into every hole in the ocean'. A lively motion at sea can be very tiring.

A Canadian singlehander who made an Atlantic crossing from Southern Ireland to the West Indies in 1952, calling

Vito Dumas' *Lehg II*

Length 31ft 2in.
Beam 10ft 9in.
Moulded depth 5ft 7in.
Mainsail 215 sq.ft
Mizzen 77 sq.ft
Staysail 80 sq.ft
Jib 82 sq.ft

**The Argentine-born
Vito Dumas made many
long solo passages. In
1942-3 he rounded the
world singlehanded in
the 30ft ketch-rigged
'Lehg'. Here he is seen
aboard at Cape Town**

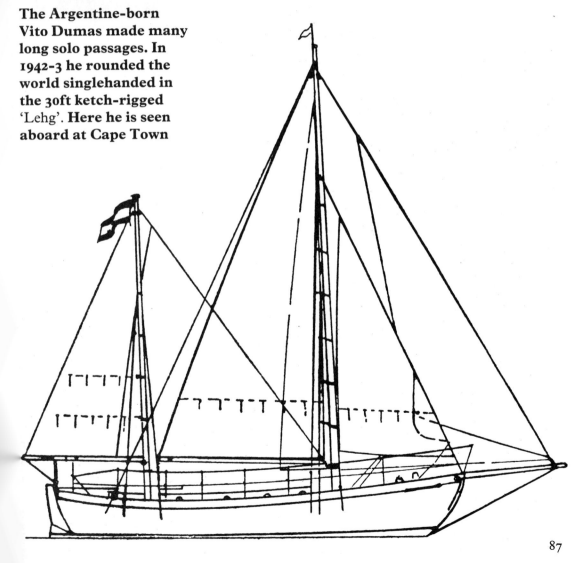

Dr Alain Bombard made a solo Atlantic crossing in an inflatable raft, of which a model is shown here, to prove that a man can live off the sea, drinking saltwater and eating fish, sea birds and plankton

en route at Las Palmas, was Dr Joseph Cunningham in *Icebird*. In 1949 the voyage from Gibraltar to New York of British solo-sailor Edward Allcard in the 34ft yawl-rigged *Temptress* drew press attention afterwards, since on the return passage he discovered a charming stowaway on board. Few singlehanders are blessed with such good fortune! But the publicity eclipsed to some extent what had been a fine solo passage made by a man who has since made many others, including a singlehanded rounding of Cape Horn. His books include *Singlehanded Passage, Temptress Returns* and *Voyage Alone*. Like Dumas, Gerbault and

Moitessier, Allcard is a real ocean wanderer.

Two Frenchmen who made singlehanded circumnavigations in the late 1950s were Marcel Bardiaux and Jean Gau. The latter, who became a naturalized American, sailed the 35ft ketch *Atom* from New York via Panama, Tahiti, New Guinea, Durban, the Azores and Gibraltar. He lingered for nine months in Tahiti, and the whole voyage took from 1953 to 1957. Jean was fifty-one years old when he started.

The other Frenchman, Marcel Bardiaux, sailed from Le Havre in France back to Le Havre via Cape Horn, Valparaiso, Tahiti (what Frenchman can resist Tahiti?), New Zealand, Durban, Cape of Good Hope, the Antilles and New York. The yacht, a 28ft sloop which he had built and called *Les Quatre Vents,* was wrecked in New Caledonia, but after repairs Bardiaux was able to complete the circumnavigation. The voyage lasted from 1950 to 1958.

At the very end of the 1950s, on a long round-world voyage from 1959 to 1964, the Norwegian-born, American naturalized, Peter Tangvald sailed the yacht *Dorothea,* partly singlehanded and partly with a crew. *Dorothea* was cutter-rigged and some 30ft in length.

5

THE COMPETITIVE ERA
Racing since 1960

Sitting up to windward, lee rail awash, is Geoffrey Williams, British winner of the 1968 singlehanded Transatlantic race, seen here aboard the victorious boat, ketch-rigged 'Sir Thomas Lipton'

T HE DECADE of the 1960s saw the first single-handed one-stop circumnavigation, the first non-stop solo circumnavigation and the beginning of singlehanded long-distance racing in earnest. The first event in the latter category occurred in 1960, when five men raced across the Atlantic. The winner of this race was Francis Chichester, who had previously made his name as an intrepid airman and had had a few years experience of ocean racing when he heard about the race. A notice had been put on the board of the Royal Ocean Racing Club. The original instigator of the race was a Colonel of the Royal Marines, 'Blondie' Hasler, a man of considerable ocean racing experience. His idea was that the race, by compelling the competitors—being singlehanded—to devise ways and means of simplifying their gear etc., would help to simplify sailing. This race and those which followed it are discussed later in this chapter, so it will suffice at this point merely to mention the races chronologically in order to place them in this picture of the general development of singlehanded sailing.

This first race was sponsored by the British newspaper, the *Observer*, as was the second race in 1964 which attracted much more notice in the press. On this occasion the *Guardian* newspaper signed Chichester and also Dr David Lewis to radio progress reports daily. The *Daily Mail* signed Mike Ellison, and the *Daily Express* was relying upon Val Howells. After the first race both Chichester and Lewis had written books, and the public had become much more interested in the idea; so had the international yachting fraternity, as we shall see later. There were fourteen finishers, the race being won by Frenchman Eric Tabarly.

The third *Observer* singlehanded race, which took place in 1968, was a completely international event and still bigger, there being nineteen finishers. In 1972 no fewer than forty yachts finished, and by this time it was clear that the singlehanded trans-Atlantic had acquired all the prestige of a classic international race, held at intervals of four years.

Francis Chichester started in the 1972 race, but as we shall see later had to retire. But in 1966-7 he was to set an example which has had tremendous repercussions; he decided to sail to Australia and back to England, singlehanded, with only one stop at Sydney. Moreover, he was out to race against the time taken for the passage by the famous wool clippers of the last great days of sail.

For this a special boat was commissioned, and designers Angus Primrose and Captain John Illingworth, a man of enormous ocean racing experience and knowhow, produced the swift, beautiful and controversial *Gypsy Moth IV*. The size of this boat, her design, her relatively narrow beam, all made for speed, and it was speed which Chichester sought. But they also made the boat uncomfortable, inclined to steep angles of heel, and exhausting over long periods. In spite of this the circumnavigation was a tremendous success. Nobody had come anywhere near the speed of Chichester's voyage; he made Sydney in one-hundred and seven days, and although this was over the one-hundred days taken by the really fast clippers it was well within the average time taken by many of them. Moreover, Chichester's self-steering gear was lost on passage, a fact which emphasizes greatly the determination of this extraordinary man to race his boats as fast as possible, self-steering or not, sleep or not! This determination to race is always evident. After winning the 1960 race across the Atlantic Chichester, not content with this, felt that he could better the time taken: in 1962 he accordingly sailed again across the Atlantic, entirely alone, to race against his own time of forty days, eleven hours and thirty minutes. And he won, making the crossing in just over thirty-three days: an improvement of a week!

On his circumnavigation, having taken a very necessary period of rest at Sydney where certain modifications were made to *Gypsy Moth IV*, Francis Chichester, although advised by many to call it a day, carried on to round Cape Horn and complete the circumnavigation, surviving a 'knock-down' in the Tasman Sea and finally arriving at Plymouth after sunset to an unprecedented welcome covered by television and radio and seen and heard by millions. The extraordinarily emotional reception was Nelsonian in its intensity and sincerity. For Chichester the voyage meant an ambition realized and a knighthood; for thousands of his countrymen and women it was an inspiration.

Competing in the 1964 trans-Atlantic race was a Portsmouth yachtsman, a grocer, by the name of Alec Rose. It was his first attempt at the race and he achieved the

David Lewis aboard
'Cardinal Vertue', **the 5-
ton sloop in which he
entered for the 1960
race**

satisfaction of coming in fourth, making the crossing in thirty-six days. Encouraged by this, he decided to sail round the world. His boat, unlike *Gypsy Moth IV* which had been designed for the job by a team of skilled naval architects, was a homely yawl of 36ft overall length and 31ft on the waterline, built in Calcutta in 1948. However, in one respect Rose's vessel shared something with *Gypsy Moth IV*, for John Illingworth and Sir David Mackworth had completely re-rigged her for the 1964 trans-Atlantic race. For this race she was rigged as a cutter, but for the circumnavigation the mast was lengthened and a small mizzen mast added, thus converting the vessel into a yawl. Although her new rig with its high-aspect-ratio mainsail and typical Illingworth sail plan looked modern enough, the hull retained an unpretentious and somewhat old-fashioned appearance; this was the typical boat of the impecunious cruising yachtsman. Together with her owner, she was perfectly cast for her role. Her name, striking the right note of homeliness and lack of pomp, was *Lively Lady*. For what gave Rose's voyage and his subsequent knighthood its great popular interest was the fact that this circumnavigation was made by an ordinary man in an elderly, ordinary boat, unsponsored and—to begin with— unsung.

Alec Rose, who was born in 1908 in Canterbury in Kent, had little or no connection with the sea until he joined the Royal Naval Volunteer Reserve in the Second World War, in which he served on Atlantic convoy duty. Like many another the navy and the sea left its mark on him, and after the war he took up sailing. Although the trans-Atlantic race was his first deep-water venture, he had some time previously been dreaming of a voyage round the world.

The adventure met with disaster right at the start. In the early hours of the morning in the English Channel near Ushant, *Lively Lady* was struck by a steamship, breaking the yacht's bowsprit, two guard-rail stanchions, and other gear on the mast. Repairs at sea were out of the question, and the disconsolate Rose put back to Plymouth. At Mashford's yard inspection revealed that repairs would not take as long as he had feared, and Rose went to bed ashore in a happier frame of mind.

However, next morning brought the dreadful news that at low water the yacht had fallen away from the wall heavily on to her side, cracking timbers and suffering damage that would take weeks to repair. This time postponement of the voyage was inevitable, for it would be well into October before she was repaired and this would have meant being off Cape Horn in midwinter.

It was gall and wormwood for Rose. On Friday 26 August, Francis Chichester arrived for his start round the world on the 27th, and Rose recounts how he went on board *Gypsy Moth IV* for a drink with Chichester. He also commented on the apparent absence of handholds, visualizing being thrown about in heavy weather.

Rose's second start was made in July of the following year. This time he was successful, reaching Melbourne after surviving many gales and at one point almost being dismasted. After leaving Melbourne, seen off by a huge crowd, he ran into more bad weather and was forced to call at Bluff Harbour in New Zealand. The steel fitting at the mainmast head had parted. Under conditions of extreme difficulty he made Bluff, and a new masthead fitting was flown there personally by Sir David Mackworth. The job done, Rose continued his circumnavigation, rounding the Horn at midday on 1 April. As Rose himself said, it was an 'April Fool's Day' he would never forget! 'I stood and stared at that great hump of land . . . it was the moment', he said 'that I had dreamed about and planned for.'

Although it is inevitable that to the reader the rest of the voyage should seem something of an anti-climax, to the lone sailor it is anything but, as gale succeeds gale, accident succeeds accident and one is aware of the many thousands of miles still to be covered. Shortly after rounding the Horn, Rose's automatic steering gear needed urgent repairs, and it continued to give trouble afterwards. But through difficulties, calms, and fickle winds alternating with gales, he made it, reaching Portsmouth where a tremendous welcome awaited him. Like Chichester, he was knighted by Her Majesty Queen Elizabeth II. From Portsmouth it had taken Alec Rose 354 days. Compared with Chichester's 274 from Plymouth to Plymouth that was slow, but *Lively Lady* was no racer. With little money and no sponsorship, Alec Rose had fulfilled a life's ambition and given inspiration to millions. It was an achievement to be pleased about.

In 1962, the year that Sir Francis Chichester made his second solo trans-Atlantic crossing, a Japanese named Kenichi Horie sailed from Osaka to San Francisco in ninety-four days, right across the Pacific ocean, in a 19ft boat. It was the intention of his father, a business man, that Horie should go to university, but Horie had other ideas. Obsessed with the notion of a Pacific crossing, he went about training himself for the task with the thoroughness and tenacity of purpose we have come to associate with the Japanese people. He had learned to sail as a boy, studied charts and weather maps and learned English. When he left school his savings from work (in his father's motor car business) were carefully put by, and all with the one intention of buying a boat in which to cross the Pacific singlehanded.

It is a remarkable story of determination. The fact that the boat he eventually bought was only 19ft long was due primarily to financial reasons. At the age of twenty-three, he had saved about £500 (about $1250), and this would not pay for anything larger. The Japanese naval architect Yokoyama had designed a 19-footer with a beam of 6ft 7in. which £500 would build. Sails, for which Horie had no money left, came from a friend.

Nineteen feet is very small for a boat in which to cross the Pacific. With boats of such a size conditions will be cramped and the motion lively when the winds blow fiercely. The storage of food, water and other essentials is also a problem. Horie gave considerable thought to such problems, which is not to imply that other long-distance solo sailors have not done the same, but with a vessel so small the problem intensifies. Kenichi Horie's calculations, taking into account the fact that some of his liquid would come from tinned fruit and canned beer, were sufficiently accurate to leave him just $2\frac{1}{2}$ gallons of fresh water when he reached San Francisco!

In May 1962 Horie and *Mermaid*, as his boat was called, left Osaka. It was a quiet departure with no publicity. Deliberately. He recounted his remarkable crossing afterwards in a book, the English version of which is entitled *Sailing Alone Across the Pacific*. When he arrived in America he was lucky in that the US Customs and Immigration gave him a visitor's visa for a thirty-day stay. Lucky because he had no passport! He had not applied for one in Japan fearing that the necessary revelation of his destination and method of travel might have prejudiced his chances of going at all. So, typically, he sailed without a passport; the risk of not going was greater than the risk of

Kenichi Horie's *Mermaid*

Length 19ft 1·5in.
Waterline length 16ft 6in.
Beam 6ft 7in.
Draft 3ft 7in.
Mainsail 85·5 sq.ft
Cruising jib 51·3 sq.ft
Storm jib 28·9 sq.ft
Staysails 53·3 sq.ft
Trisail 27·5 sq.ft
Fin keel 650 lbs

MERMAID

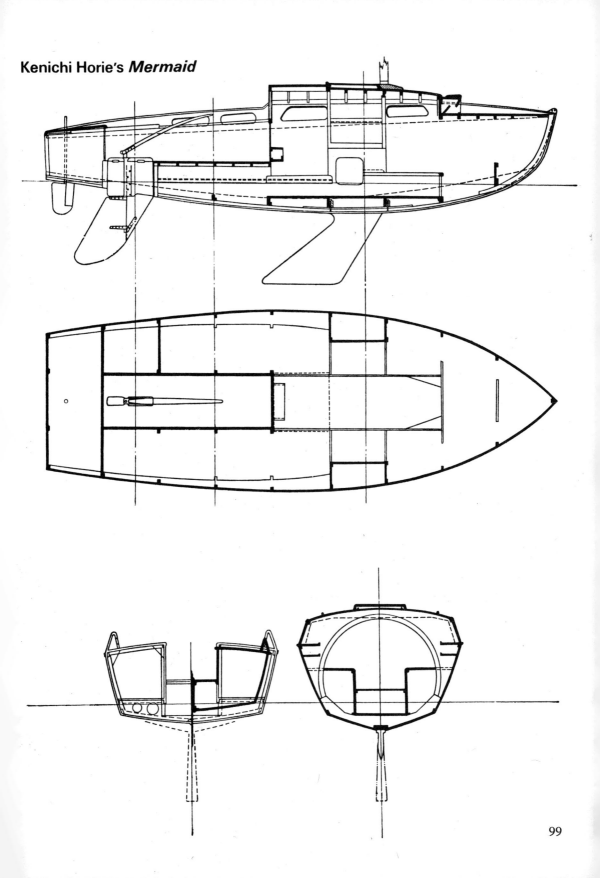

Kenichi Horie's *Mermaid*

99

Perspective drawing of the *Mermaid* showing parts of hull and rigging

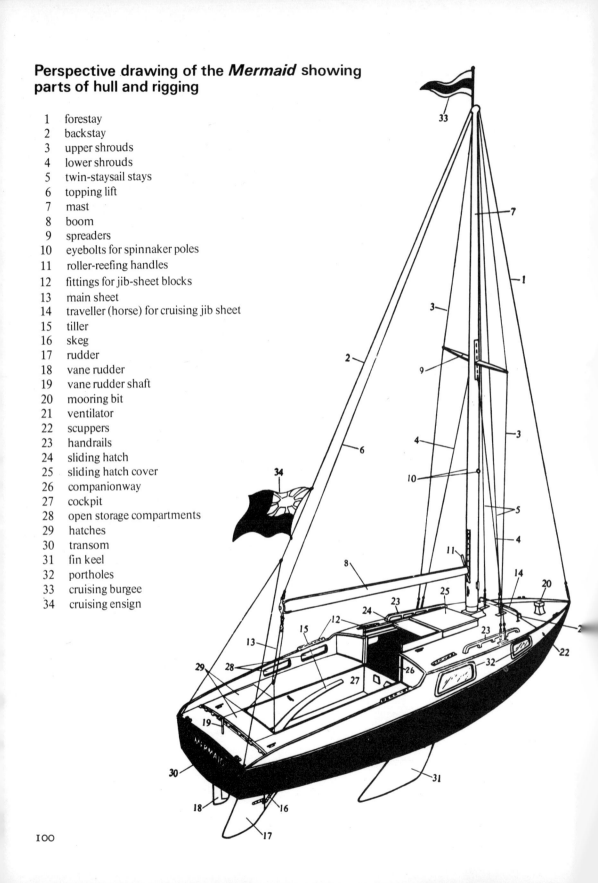

not being able to land the other side. He was of course properly ticked off when he got back to Japan, but they also gave him the welcome that his courage deserved. A credit to his country and to sailing folk the world over, he had more than deserved it.

The youngest sailor (at the time of writing) to have sailed the world singlehanded is Robin Lee Graham, an American. At the age of sixteen, on 27 July 1965, he sailed from San Pedro in California, in *Dove*, a 24ft fibre-glass Lapwing sloop, bought by his father (who had originally taught Robin to sail and favoured the project), who helped him to fit out for the voyage. Original cost of boat was $5500; final cost after fitting out and provisioning was $8000. Robin Graham's long voyage took him five years. It was a voyage of many stops and incidents which are vividly described in the book *Dove*, by Robin himself with Derek Gill. This saga (which includes the meeting and marrying of a beautiful young American girl in the South Seas) has a tremendous message for young people. One has to remind oneself in reading that Robin was only sixteen at the start! (Gregory Peck has produced a film *The Dove* about it.) Although interesting for its revealing accounts of fear and loneliness and of losing a mast, getting swept overboard and other adventures of the sort, which test the courage of men and women of any age, it is the appealing accounts of despair, alternating with the invigoratingly youthful attitude to the whole business of sea voyaging, that makes this book so valuable.

One of the results of the heroic solo-one-stop circumnavigations of Chichester and Rose was the first singlehanded race, non-stop, round the world. This was won by a young English ex-Merchant Navy man called Robin Knox-Johnston. A remark of his father's ('that's about all there's left to do now'), referring to the possibility of a solo circumnavigation completely non-stop, kept turning in Knox-Johnston's mind. The idea took root, but Knox-Johnston was not the only one who had been struck with it. In fact by the end of 1967, at least two other yachtsmen were planning the same voyage: Commander Bill Leslie King and Captain John Ridgway. By February of 1968 the London *Sunday Times* had come out with their offer of a trophy, the Golden Globe, for the winner of a non-stop singlehanded race. Another seaman of experience and repute had joined the lists, Bernard Moitessier of France.

The final list included two trimarans, those of Commander Nigel Tetley and the ill-fated Donald Crowhurst.

Knox-Johnston finished the course without rule-infringement in ten and a half months. It was a magnificent achievement and a triumph over difficulties and he was awarded the CBE. The race itself made history in a number of ways.

A circumnavigation of considerable interest was that in 1970 of Chay Blyth (the ex-paratrooper who in 1966 had rowed across the Atlantic with John Ridgway in ninety-two days)—a remarkable circumnavigation in that in the yacht *British Steel* Blyth, sailing against the prevailing winds and currents, made the longest windward voyage in yachting history, a passage from port to port of 292 days.

In choosing to sail against the great westerly winds that blow south of latitude 40° south, Chay Blyth was deliberately setting himself a particularly tough proposition. His reason for so doing was simple: no one had ever done it before. Such a voyage needed a tough man and a tough boat. Blyth is a tough man. Born in Hawick in Scotland, he joined the Parachute Regiment at eighteen and served abroad, including Aden. It was in 1966 that he and Captain John Ridgway also of the Parachute Regiment, rowed the Atlantic, a feat for which Blyth was awarded the British Empire Medal. In 1967 he left the army, and in the following year competed in the *Sunday Times* sponsored Golden Globe race. However, he had to give up and this, as we have already seen in Chapter 1, led to his non-stop circumnavigation in *British Steel*.

The yacht was tough too: 59ft long overall, she had a beam of 12ft 10in. and displaced 17 tons when fully loaded. The area of her working sails amounted to almost 1500 square feet—a very large sail area for a singlehander. *British Steel* is a curious name for a yacht, but there was good reason for this since Blyth was championed in his undertaking by the British Steel Corporation. This was, in fact a case of sponsorship at its best, especially since Blyth's main champion on the Board, W. F. Cartwright, was himself an experienced yachtsman.

British Steel was designed by British naval architect Robert Clark, from whose drawing board so many beautiful and successful little ships have come. Chay Blyth and *British Steel* rounded the Horn at Christmas, in point of fact on 24 December. The Horn lived up to its reputation and produced gale force 8 to 9 on Christmas Day. Blyth recalled that the seas there had 'a quality of sheer bigness that was new and menacing'. At one point, he was thrown right across the cockpit, cutting his forehead. Although the boat rode the big seas well their sheer size was continually stopping her dead. Blyth could not get her to sail any closer to the wind than 60°, and for the first time he was fully aware of what it meant to sail against the system. He doubted, he said, if he had ever felt more miserable in his life.

In fact, however, it was not the Horn that provided the worst gale of the voyage. This occurred some 1500 miles from Cape Town and forced Blyth miles off course. He recalls how on leaving Tasmania he felt, although he was still only half-way round, that there was a different feel to the voyage. He felt in a way like being homeward bound. So it was all the more unpalatable when in the latter part of April he encountered a storm of such viciousness and power that he wrote of it 'if I ever dream, I'll dream of this storm,' and admits that for the first time in his life he was genuinely frightened.

Frightened he may have been, but his courage and determination never faltered. To have made this voyage with a competent crew would have been a fine achievement, to have done it singlehanded compels admiration.

We have already seen that from time to time long singlehanded passages have been made in very small boats. One that must surely be included here is that of an American, who not only sailed a 13½ft boat across the Atlantic by himself, but was forty-seven years old when he did it! In fact he had his forty-seventh birthday at sea on the passage. The boat was forty years old and was called *Tinkerbelle*, and her skipper was Robert Manry.

Although he had wanted to own a boat for many years, Manry did not do so until he was over forty. The principal reason was finance, and the boat he bought was very modest, costing only $160. She was almost thirty-five years old when he bought her, and was badly in need of repair.

So Manry began his sailing career as a shipwright. He had some knowledge of carpentry and the use of tools, and in less than a year he had a seaworthy boat and could begin sailing. With his wife and two children he was able to experience the pleasures of lake sailing. Anyone observing the man at this time, a sub-editor on the Cleveland

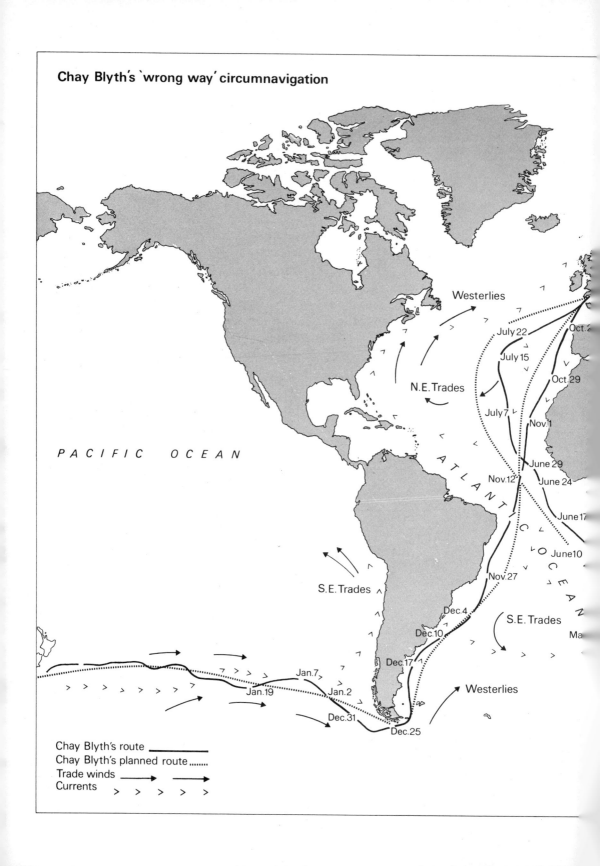

Chay Blyth's 'wrong way' circumnavigation

Westerlies

N.E. Trades

PACIFIC OCEAN

ATLANTIC OCEAN

July 22

July 15

July 7

Oct. 2

Oct. 29

Nov. 1

June 29

June 24

June 17

June 10

Nov. 12

Nov. 27

S.E. Trades

Dec. 4

Dec. 10

Dec. 17

S.E. Trades

Ma

Jan. 7

Jan. 2

Jan. 19

Dec. 31

Dec. 25

Westerlies

Chay Blyth's route —————
Chay Blyth's planned route ·······
Trade winds ⟶   ⟶
Currents >   >   >   >   >

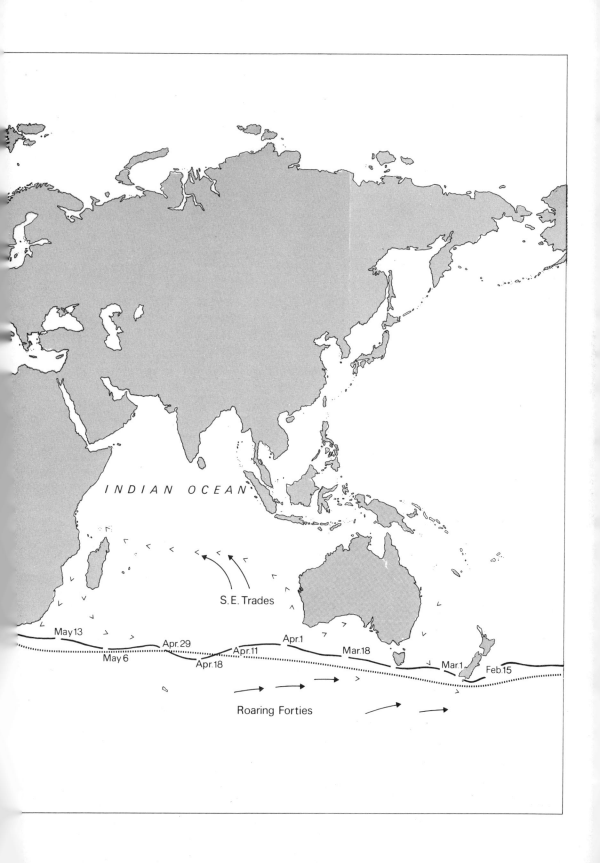

INDIAN OCEAN

S.E. Trades

May 13

May 6

Apr. 29

Apr. 18

Apr. 11

Apr. 1

Mar. 18

Mar. 1

Feb. 15

Roaring Forties

newspaper *Plain Dealer* with a small boat for family sailing, would never have guessed that one day he would sail solo across the Atlantic. He added a cabin to *Tinkerbelle* in 1962 and made certain improvements. A much more ambitious cruise of seventy-five miles resulted on Lake Erie and he continued to get useful but relatively modest sailing experience.

One now gets an inkling of the stuff Manry was really made of when, on a friend proposing that he should join a 25ft boat sailing the Atlantic to England, he immediately agreed. Plans were made but the friend changed his mind. But not Manry. He was going, and the only way he could now go was in *Tinkerbelle*. He made a test cruise of some 200 miles on Lake Erie, bought navigational instruction books and an Air Force sextant and practised taking sights in the garden. The whole thing fairly oozes amateurism: the ideal of the Corinthian effortlessly overriding all difficulties. No wonder John Anderson included Robert Manry in his great book on the *Ulysses Factor*!

But the planning was by no means amateur and calculations were made to a nicety. Like Kenichi Horie, the very minuteness of Manry's boat presented considerable problems of storage and provisioning. When he finally landed at Falmouth he found he was famous. There is to the public something fascinating about an ordinary family man suddenly undertaking a hazardous voyage in a very small boat. Of course opinions are as many, varied and diverse as the winds that blow over the sea, but most people recognized and responded to the cheerful courage and pleasing modesty of the man. Neither skipper nor boat were youngsters, and in a way this added to the magic. Robert Manry had long had a dream. He wanted to make it come true, and he did.

A very fast record-breaking circumnavigation with one stop (Sydney) was made in 1974 by French singlehander Alain Colas, a yachtsman of enormous experience, particularly in singlehanded racing. He took fifty-seven days less than Sir Francis Chichester to sail the same course. The boat, called *Manureva*, was a trimaran (three hulls), capable of very high speeds. She had been renamed, her original name being *Pen Duick IV*, a product of the genius of Eric Tabarly.

Colas had his fair share of trouble. Almost at the start he was practically asphyxiated by a gas leak while asleep in the cabin. He inevitably encountered very severe weather, but having been blessed with relative calm round the Horn he became a prey to the dreadful desolation of that region, and suffered for two days from loneliness, depression and, as he admits, real fear. From the Equator to the Azores he set up a new record of thirteen days, and in so doing almost equalled the speed of the fabled clipper *Cutty Sark,* another Chichester ambition. Colas and Chichester would appear to have much in common. The Frenchman is at the time of writing planning another attack on the trans-Atlantic. Like Chichester he sails alone but he sails against others or against a time schedule. It is as if he has taken up the torch fallen from the hand of the gallant captain of *Gypsy Moth*. Returning to Dinard on 28 March 1974, Alain Colas' fast circumnavigation delighted his count-rymen, and M. Yvon Bourges, deputy mayor of Dinard, was amply justified in bestowing on the black-bearded sailor the freedom of the city.

The racing element in single-handed sailing, first significantly apparent in 1960, nowadays features so prominently that it is appropriate to examine at this point its birth and growth in rather more depth. From 1876, when American fisherman Alfred Johnson sailed *Centen-nial* across the Atlantic Ocean, a great company of gallant men and women made long solo voyages. But very few of them raced. Not until Francis Chichester, with the Damoclean sword of grave illness over his head, discussed the idea with Blondie Hasler, does anyone appear to have thought about organized singlehanded racing.

It would seem that just to get there was in itself a sufficient challenge in the pre-First World War days. Later, as yachts improved in design and gear and as more long-distance solo passages were made, one might have expected to find more of the competitive element. Not so. Harry Pidgeon didn't want to race anybody; nor did Alain Gerbault, nor Alain Bombard, nor Ann Davison in 1952. It was left to ocean-racing enthusiast and 'Cockleshell hero' of World War II, Hasler, to put a notice on the board of the Royal Ocean Racing Club and for Francis Chichester and three other like-minded spirits to get the whole business started as recently as 1960. Hasler maintained that such a race would get rid of some of the chores of sailing, since those competing would have to find new ways and means to simplify their boats' gear.

Bill Howell up foreward in 'Golden Cockerel'. Howell had sailed 'Star Drift' to sixth place in the 1964 Transatlantic race; with the new 43ft catamaran shown here he challenged in the 1968 race and came fifth

This was a laudable enough concept. But I wonder! Colonel Hasler had had an impressive record in ocean racing under tough conditions and was an inveterate competitor. Francis Chichester had been breaking records in planes for years and was another for whom competition was the spice of life. I do not doubt that they did think that the race would improve yachts' gear etc., but I feel certain that the real idea was to *race*.

There are some people who must race, for whom just to get there is dull. Once the idea of singlehanded racing caught on, the size and scope of the races grew like jungle foliage. The only surprising factor is that the sport of singlehanded yacht racing took so long to arrive.

That first race in fact attracted enquiries from all over the world. From France, Denmark, the USA, Canada and Germany came requests for information as soon as it had been announced that a race would start from Plymouth on 11 June. There were many enquiries from Britain also. Yet only eight firm entries made up the total as the starting date drew near, and of these eight only five actually sailed. The competing yachts were: *Gypsy Moth III*, Francis Chichester's 39ft yawl; *Jester*, a Folkboat rigged with a Chinese (junk type) lugsail, which was Colonel Hasler's entry; *Cardinal Vertue*, a Vertue class sloop, the entry of Dr David Lewis; another Folkboat belonging to Val Howells, called *Eira;* and Frenchman Jean Lacombe's *Cap Horn*, a centre-board sloop. The Vertue and the two Folkboats were 25-footers and *Cap Horn*, the smallest, was only 21ft long. The French entrant had been ordered by a yachtsman in New York, and Jean Lacombe was delivering it by racing there! Favourite for the race was the ocean racer *Gypsy Moth III*, sailed by the fifty-eight-year-old Francis Chichester.

In Chapter 6, in examining the wind systems and currents of the world, we shall see the effect of winds and currents on a sailor's choice of route. The routes which the entrants for the historic 1960 Atlantic race elected to take are interesting to compare. Look at the chart overpage where the courses of the five entrants are traced. It will be seen that Hasler took the northernmost route, his object being to avoid if possible the depressions of the North Atlantic. Lewis and Chichester took the Great Circle, the shortest route. Howell's route in *Eira* was more southerly, while Jean Lacombe took the most southerly route of all, that to the Azores, hoping to avoid the windward work which would doubtless present a problem to the Great Circle sailors. The chart shows their progress, and how Chichester emerged the winner when he reached New York on 21 July after being at sea for 40½ days. The routes of the other competitors stop at 21 June to show the progress they had made by the time Chichester crossed the finishing line. The actual finishing times of the other four were in order of arrival: *Jester*, 30 June (forty-eight days at sea); *Cardinal Vertue*, 6 July (fifty-six days at sea); *Eira*, 13 July (sixty-three days); and the little *Cap Horn* eventually turned up on 24 July after seventy-four days en route.

The race not only proved that it was possible to have such a contest without casualties, but also that self-steering gear of some sort was an enormous boon. Hasler was himself the inventor of one type of self-steering gear. There are now two principal types: the pendulum-servo type of vane gear, and the trim-tab type in which the wind

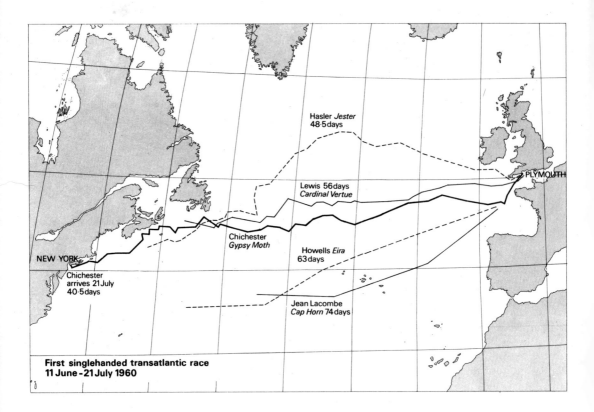

Hasler *Jester*
48·5 days

Lewis 56 days
Cardinal Vertue

PLYMOUTH

Chichester
Gypsy Moth

Howells *Eira*
63 days

NEW YORK

Chichester
arrives 21 July
40·5 days

Jean Lacombe
Cap Horn 74 days

**First singlehanded transatlantic race
11 June - 21 July 1960**

vane turns a small rudder (the trim-tab) which is itself hung on the trailing edge of the rudder. In this first race, self-steering devices proved thoroughly workable and Colonel Hasler reported that he had had to be personally at the helm of his boat *Jester* for only one hour of the entire voyage. There had been a number of setbacks: David Lewis in *Cardinal Vertue* had had to put back into Plymouth to repair a damaged mast, setting off again on 13 June; Val Howells in *Eira* had to put into Bermuda to get a new battery and chronometer, and little *Cap Horn* had to be taken in tow for an hour or two near the American coast on account of very bad weather.

The next *Observer*-sponsored race, which took place in 1964, attracted a great deal more attention. Both Chichester and Lewis had written excellent books (*Alone Across the Atlantic* and *The Ship that Would Not Travel Due West*, respectively). And in 1962 Francis Chichester had made a well-publicized second Atlantic crossing, racing (and beating) his time in 1960. For the 1964 race both Chichester and Lewis were signed up by the *Guardian* to send in daily progress reports by radio. Val Howells was reporting for the *Daily Express*. A new entrant, Miles Ellison, had been signed up by the *Daily Mail*, and the *Observer*, original sponsor of the race, was certain to give it a good deal of space. This time too, there was a more international flavour. As well as Jean Lacombe (with another 21-footer called *Golif*), there was his compatriot Lieutenant Eric Tabarly of the French Navy in a 44ft ketch called *Pen Duick II*. There were Australian Bill Howell and Dane Axel Pederson, the former sailing *Stardrift* and the latter *Marco Polo*. David Lewis was there again and another newcomer was Alec Rose in *Lively Lady*. Lewis sailed *Rehu Moana*, a multi-hull which was actually ineligible, under the rules, for the handicap award. Other multi-hulls were *Folatre* sailed by Derek Kelsall, and *Misty Miller*, the entry of Michael Butterfield. Hasler was there again with *Jester*, as was Val Howells with a boat called *Akka*; also among the original five was Francis Chichester in *Gypsy Moth III*. Geoffrey Chaffey was a newcomer sailing *Eric 2*, as was Bob Bunker in *Vanda Caelea*; finally there was the 41ft *Tammie Norie* sailed by Doctor Robin McCurdy, who had the bad luck to retire. The others all finished the race, the first five placings being 1st, *Pen Duick II;* 2nd, *Gypsy Moth III;* 3rd, *Akka;* 4th,

Lively Lady; and 5th, *Jester.*

This was the shape of things to come. Of the old guard, Howells and Hasler both aquitted themselves more than honourably. In second and fourth places came the two men who later were to be knighted by Queen Elizabeth II for their singlehanded circumnavigation of the world, and in the winner Eric Tabarly there emerged a fanatic exponent of long-distance racing, destined to make a formidable impact upon the sport; his elapsed time of 27 days 3 hours and 56 minutes was remarkable. His boat *Pen Duick II* was designed and built especially for the race. A ketch-rigged boat, constructed in plywood for lightness, she was full of innovations which were Tabarly's pet hobby: a wheel like that of a car, a perspex dome over the cockpit, roller gear for the spinnaker halliard and the ability to set an impressive variety of sail combinations on her two masts. Her master was no less eye-catching. Thirty-two years of age and an officer in the French Navy, Tabarly was a stocky Breton only 5ft 4in. in height, and as Bretons so often seem to be he was, in the words of Francis Chichester, as tough as old boots. Tabarly had made a thorough study of the course in all its aspects and he and his boat were at a pitch of training and readiness to rival an Olympic athlete. It was the forerunner of the Gallic challenge that was to be so victorious in the 1972 race when the French took the first three places.

Equally determined, Francis Chichester had had *Gypsy Moth III* re-rigged by expert John Illingworth. The smallest boat in the race was, once again, that of Jean Lacombe; *Golif* was built in glass-reinforced plastics. There was another significant factor in the appearance in the race of three multi-hulls, those of David Lewis, whose boat *Rehu Moana,* Maori for *Sea Spray,* was a catamaran (twin hulls); Derek Kelsall, an oil engineer whose boat *Folatre* was a trimaran (three hulls); and lawyer Michael Butterfield, whose entry *Misty Miller* was another catamaran. The controversial subject of multi versus mono hull had entered the singlehander arena.

This second race not only drew a much bigger entry than the first, the boats themselves were bigger, three being over 40ft in overall length and the majority being over 30ft. The largest was the impressive *Pen Duick II* measuring 44ft overall. Quite different from the sleek thoroughbreds was the 30ft cutter *Lively Lady* sailed by fifty-five-year-old

Portsmouth fruit merchant Alec Rose. But Rose, an ex-RNVR officer, was no novice where the North Atlantic was concerned and handled his beloved old ship with competence and style to make a creditable thirty-six days passage.

With this race, many of the originator 'Blondie' Hasler's ideas came into being, perhaps especially with Tabarly's boat with its labour-saving devices and obvious efficiency. Hasler himself was to write in the *Observer* that Eric's performance in getting her to the Brenton Reef in twenty seven days, in spite of an unserviceable vane steering gear, must rank very near the summit of singlehanded sailing. There is no doubt that every word of this is true and Hasler had reason to be pleased, but as is bound to happen in competitive sports, with Tabarly singlehanded yacht racing had entered a new phase of professionalism and dedication.

In 1968 there was a third race, which brought still more innovations. For one thing the controversial subject of sponsorship made its appearance. And there were still more boats: eyecatching among the favourites was the new entry of Eric Tabarly, *Pen Duick IV*, a 67ft-long trimaran with the remarkable beam of 35ft! Another large boat was *Sir Thomas Lipton*, at 57ft long, the entry of Geoffrey Williams; she had been designed by Robert Clark (who was to design *British Steel* for Chay Blyth) and built specially for the race. None of the original singlehanders of the 1960 race entered, although Hasler's yacht *Jester* was there, sailed by Michael Richey who had bought her. Bill Howell, who had sailed *Star Drift* to sixth place in 1964, was there with a new boat, a catamaran 43ft in length called *Golden Cockerel*.

The name of Howell's catamaran reflects the sponsorship in part of the brewing firm of John Courage, whose symbol is a cockerel, and several other entrants had some degree of sponsorship. *Spirit of Cutty Sark*, sailed into fourth place by Leslie Williams, was backed by Cutty Sark whisky. The 45ft trimaran *Gancia Girl*, sailed by Martin Minter-Kemp, was backed by the Italian wine firm of Gancia. The British brewing house of Watneys sponsored another trimaran, *Startled Faun*, sailed by Colin Forbes. And the favourite, Eric Tabarly, had his expenses paid by the French Navy.

Yet there were plenty who were there for the love of the

game and at their own expense. There was *Atlantis III*, a 27ft-long sloop-rigged boat sailed by David Pyle and built by him in marine plywood. There was *Rob Roy*, a 32ft ketch sailed by Stephen Pakenham, a Sussex clergyman, and another 32-footer was sloop-rigged *Opus*, sailed by Brian Cooke, a bank manager. A new and welcome feature was the entry of the twenty-six-year-old German girl Edith Baumann sailing in *Koala III*, a 39ft catamaran. It was the first time a woman had entered for the singlehand-ed race, and bad luck that her boat was lost, although Miss Baumann herself was happily rescued. There were plenty of other unspectacular boats, entries for the fun of the thing as much as for the honour and glory, yet somehow the race had changed in character. First, it now attracted a lot of public interest. Secondly, among the competing boats were some very big yachts, and this reflected the presence of the sponsor. It was inevitable that those sailing the sponsored yachts were sailing now under very different kinds of pressure. Geoffrey Williams, who in *Sir Thomas Lipton* was to sail the course in the shortest elapsed time, wrote afterwards in his book *Separate Horizons:* 'This race would stretch me continuously, never letting me relax, never letting me forget the hundreds of people who had put energy, money, and trust in *Lipton*, never letting his bows look away from Newport, USA.' Tabarly's dedication and thoroughness were to be found equally in Williams. He had made it known before the race that courses would be radioed to him from London, having been worked out by computer and based on his position at the time, all available data regarding weather conditions, likely wind shifts, etc.

To many people all this seemed to be turning the race into a computer-controlled, ocean-crossing project similar to a space journey monitored from Cape Kennedy. Indeed, the radioed information not only helped Williams to avoid a very bad storm but he did, in fact, come in first. Subsequent races, and indeed events in this 1968 race, have shown that such aids are no substitute for good seamanship and the plain guts needed to keep the boat tramping along at her best speed. Nevertheless on the fateful day of 10 June a storm blew up, catching the leading boats. The wind freshened steadily, gusting up to hurricane force. Howell's *Golden Cockerel*, one of the boats caught by the gale, was forced to lie a-hull (no sail set whatever) for thirty-four hours, and other leading boats were similarly affected.

Williams's computer had advised him to head north, and by the 11th, having edged round the worst of the depression, he sailed into the leading position, a position he maintained to win.

But computers cannot do everything. On 23 June, south of Newfoundland, Williams had a jammed halliard on *Lipton*'s mizzen mast and had to climb the mast to clear it. By the time he had done this he was committed to a course north of the Nantucket Light, which was contrary to the sailing regulations for the race. From Newport Williams was radioed telling him that he was taking the wrong course, and he radioed back asking for instruction. The race officer in Newport was the experienced Colonel Odling-Smee, who had the difficult choice deciding whether to send Williams back round the Nantucket Light or not. He decided not, and *Sir Thomas Lipton* carried on to win the race.

Naturally enough, this decision on the part of the race committee was the subject of much controversy after-wards. Particularly annoyed by it was South African Bruce Dalling who in *Voortrekker* was only seventeen hours behind Williams who already had a twelve-hour penalty against him. But although the *Voortrekker* trust sent a telegram complaining that Williams had broken the rules, Dalling did not protest personally. Close behind Dalling came Tom Follett with a time of 27 days 13 minutes, sailing *Cheers*, which was perhaps the strangest-looking craft of them all. She was a proa, with two 40ft-long hulls and two masts, but with no rigging to stay them on the windward hull. This boat did not tack in the ordinary way when going about, but simply reversed the sails, so that the stern became the new bow on each hull. It may have surprised a good many people that she did so well, but not those who knew of the great experience and skill of Follett.

The French, who perhaps had been a little cocksure at the start, were to have bad luck. Thirty-six hours after the start Eric Tabarly ran into a merchant ship while below brewing coffee! *Pen Duick IV* suffered damage to her starboard float and had to put back to Plymouth, and this was to put her out of the race. The trimaran *Yaksha*, with Joan de Kat at the helm, had to put into Alderney. The home-made multihull had rigging problems and later ran into serious trouble and sank. The trimaran *Tamoure*, sailed by Commander Waquet, put back into Brest. *Silvia*

II, sailed by André Foëzon, was dismasted; Foëzon put into Plymouth and resumed the race on 12 June, finishing some twenty-nine days later—a notable achievement. Finishing in tenth position, the leading French yacht was *Magnelonne;* her helmsman was Jean-Yves Terlain, who made the crossing in 38 days 9 hours and 10 minutes. In 1972 he was to make it (in a considerably larger vessel) in 21 days 5 hours and 14 minutes, and in so doing sailed into second place.

This was in the *Observer* race of 1972, a race which was to vindicate the multihull, although the 1968 race had shown the latter to be well capable of holding its own with conventional craft on long races. The other vindication was the confidence of the French, the first three places being taken by Frenchmen. The 1972 was a bigger race than ever, the thirty-eight entries of 1968 having almost doubled to make fifty-nine, although only forty-eight yachts actually started on the deadline; there were seven delayed arrivals, and three boats which did not start for various reasons beyond their control.

This time there was plenty for the world's press to write about. Sir Francis Chichester was back in the struggle with a new, Robert Clark-designed *Gypsy Moth V.* Chay Blyth's *British Steel* was there, sailed by Brian Cooke. There was a stronger female entry this time, some very personable ladies indeed! The American Tom Follett had a new boat called *Three Cheers,* one cheer presumably for each of the three hulls of this reputedly fast catamaran. The French were there in force: not Tabarly, but Tabarly's 1968 boat *Pen Duick IV* sailed by Alain Colas (who in 1974 was to make a record-breaking circumnavigation); also Jean-Marie Vidal sailing the 53ft-long trimaran *Cap 33,* Alain Gliksman's boat *Toucan,* small and slim-hulled, and Jean-Yves Terlain in *Vendredi XIII,* a three-masted schooner of 128ft overall length, the largest vessel in the race, designed by American Dick Carter. Also in the French contingent was Joel Charpentier in another schooner, the 63ft *Wild Rocket.*

There were eight multi-hull yachts and fifty-one monohulls. Among the latter, besides Colas, Follett and Vidal as already mentioned, were Philip Weld from the USA in the trimaran *Trumpeter;* two Australians, Bill Howell in his 43ft catamaran (formerly *Golden Cockerel)* now renamed *Tahiti Bill* after her owner; and journalist

Murray Sayle in *Lady of Fleet*. The French yachtsman Gerard Pestey in a 55ft trimaran *Architeuthis* and Britisher John Beswick in another trimaran, *Leen Valley Venturer*, made up the eight entrants.

Of the fifty-one mono hulls, interest tended to centre on the big yachts, of which I have already mentioned *Vendredi XIII*, the other schooner 63ft *Wild Rocket*, *Gypsy Moth V* and *British Steel*. Included among the large boats was Martin Minter-Kemp's long 65ft, narrow (10ft) schooner *Strongbow*, reputedly a flier and sponsored by Bulmers, the makers of Strongbow cider. There was also Italian yachtsman Franco Faggioni in the 50.7ft cutter *Sagittario*,

Largest entry in the 1972 race, French yacht 'Vendredi XIII', seen here surrounded by small craft, was sailed by Jean-Yves Terlain. In this race the first three places were taken by the French in a remarkable Gallic clean sweep. The huge three-master had been race favourite

American Jim Ferris in a Morgan 54 named *Whisper*, and another large boat, Dutchman Gerard Dijkstra's ocean class 71-footer, *Second Life*.

The old rule which laid down that an entering yachtsman must have sailed 500 miles to qualify was amended to the effect that the entering yacht must also have sailed the qualifying 500 miles. This was to ensure that no ill-found craft came hopefully to the starting line. The other schooners were Bruce Webb's 47.5-footer *Gazelle*, and Jock McLeod's Chinese lugsail 47ft sloop *Isles du Frioul*, Eugene Riguidel in the stainless steel-hulled 42.8ft sloop *Onyx* and Pierre Chassin's 44.3ft sloop *Concorde*.

British yachts in this group included Pat Chilton's 38ft sloop *Mary Kate of Arun*, Jock Brazier's 46ft ketch *Flying Angel*, bandleader Bob Miller's 43ft sloop *Mersea Pearl* (formerly the 1967 Fastnet race winner under the name of *Rabbit II*, sailed by her designer Dick Carter), and Peter Crowther's sixty-four-year-old gaff cutter, the 38ft *Golden Vanity*. From Italy came Ambrogio Fogar in the 38.2ft sloop *Surprise*, and completing the international flavour of this group were Belgian Oscar Debra aboard the 46ft ketch *Olva II*, Swiss Guy Piazzini in the 45.5ft ketch *Cambronne*, and Poles Zbigniew Puchalski in the 38.8ft sloop *Miranda* and Chris Baranowski in *Polonez*.

Another innovation in this race was the new trophy for boats of up to 35ft and among the yachts eligible for this was a pleasing variety of rigs and nationalities. Taking them by country of origin: from Britain came Mike McMullen, a Marine commando in a Contessa 32 called *Binkie II*, Chris Elliot in *Laurie* and John Holton in *La Bamba of Mersea* (both of them Northney 34s) and Harry Mitchell in the 33ft sloop *Mex* and Wolf Kirchner in a 32.3 footer, also sloop-rigged, called *White Dolphin*. Edoardo Cuzzetti from Italy was aboard a 32.6ft sloop *Namar IV*, and another similar-sized sloop was the 32.3 footer *White Lady* sailed by Swede Hubert Bargholtz. From the USA came the experienced Jerry Cartwright in the 32.4 footer *Scuffler III*, and from France the formidable Alain Gliksman in the 34.5 ft sloop *Toucan*.

Among the yachts over 30ft were the three lady entrants: Polish Teresa Remiszewska in her 42ft yawl *Komodor*, and two Frenchwomen, Marie Claude Fauroux in the 35ft *Aloa VII* (entered by SEB Marine de France) and Anne

Michailof in the 30.6ft sloop *P.S.*, the initials of her sponsors, Pieter Stuyvesant cigarettes (the full name not being permitted to be displayed under the rules).

Finally there were the following entrants whose yachts, measuring less than 30ft, obviously had less chance of a speedy crossing than their longer sisters, but some of which nevertheless finished in more than honourable positions in the list of final placings. For example, take the little Folkboat *Francette* of Britisher Eric Sumner who was placed thirty-first. Another Folkboat was the by-now veteran *Jester* sailed by Michael Riche. Other British entrants in this size group were Bob Salmon and Max Barton, both sailing 24.8ft Listang class sloops named *Justa Listang* and *British Fashion,* respectively. Richard Clifford entered with the 26ft Contessa-class boat *Shamaal,* actor David Blagden in the diminutive 19ft Hunter-class *Willing Griffin* and to complete the British list, Guy Hornett in the twin-keeled Kingfisher-class 26-footer *Blue Smoke,* and Andrew Spedding in the 28ft sloop *Summersong,* in which he achieved thirty-sixth place. From the USA came Robert Burn in the 28ft *Blue Gypsy,* gathering a laudable twenty-sixth place; from West Germany came Heiki Kreiger in the 29.2ft sloop *Time* in the thirty-third place. There was also Czech Richard Kinkolski in the 22.5ft yawl *Niké,* and Frenchman Gerard Curvelier in the little 21ft sloop *Tang' O.*

It was an impressive tournout of singlehanded yachtsmen, and the variety of boats and nationalities matched the varying attitudes of the contestants. For while to some like Terlain, Colas and Brian Cooke, winning was all-important, to others the fact of crossing the Atlantic singlehanded was probably sufficient. If they did well, so much the better; if they did not win any prizes it would still have been very worthwhile. It was a remarkable development from the Chichester-Hasler wager and the first *Observer* singlehanded race back in 1960. Twelve countries entered. Britain held first place in numbers with twenty-three, then came France with thirteen, America with five and Italy with four. From Poland and West Germany there were three entries each, from Australia two, and one each from Holland, Czechoslovakia, Sweden and Switzerland.

Unlike the 1968 race, the 1972 crossing provided no great storm. The majority of the contestants were thwarted by calms rather than tempests, and the most dramatic feature could be said to have been the sheer size of the fleet taking part. Of such setbacks as there were, the illness and withdrawal of Chichester shortly after the start was a disaster with which all could sympathize. And although there was no very bad weather during most of the race, yet the wind did have its casualties.

For example, Richard Kinkolski's *Niké*, the small 22ft yawl, broke her mast, as also did Max Barton's *Bristol Fashion*. The big 71-footer *Second Life* of Gerard Dijkstra lost her mainmast and *Mersea Pearl*, with Bob Miller at her helm, lost her mast at night on 10 July. Journalist Murray Sayle came to grief in his catamaran *Lady of Fleet* when the main mast broke just over 800 miles north-west of Bermuda; Bob Salmon's *Justa Listang* also lost her mast.

There were other withdrawals for various causes. Eugene Riguidel retired because of rigging trouble and Harry Mitchell's *Tuloa* developed a leak, American yachtsman Jerry Cartwright's *Scuffler III* also sprang a leak, and Cartwright put back to Falmouth soon after the start, to set sail again eventually on 27 June. Andrew Spedding was unlucky enough to have a collision in *Summersong* but, like Cartwright, was able to sail again after repairs.

One of the most traumatic dramas was that of Bill Howell aboard the catamaran *Tahiti Bill* which collided with the Russian trawler *Spika* near the Nantucket Light vessel. It was late evening and in conditions of dense fog. The port float was severely damaged at the prow, but thanks to a water-tight bulkhead the water was contained in it and the vessel suffered only from a list to port. Howell fought bravely to get the boat sailing with a mast whose rigging had been damaged as well, a persistently leaking hull, and in thick fog to boot. It was only seamanlike in the end to accept a tow from the Russian supply vessel *Flotinspekcija,* but as if all this was not enough, there was additional drama when the US Coast Guard informed Howell that a foreign vessel must not come within the statutory three-mile limit. However, a coast-guard cutter, *Point Turner,* took over the tow fifty miles off Newport!

All this shows that even with relatively calm conditions (compared with some races) a race across the Atlantic singlehanded is no pastime for the faint-hearted. But if any body or group of bodies were pleased with the result it was surely the French, who not only took the first three places in the race but collected the Royal Western Yacht Club's award for the first lady, in the attractive person of Marie Claude Fauroux in her *Aloa VII*. Of the thirteen French singlehanders who crossed the starting line, ten of them not only finished the course, but finished among the first twenty yachts home: an achievement which speaks for itself.

Alain Colas sailed a skilful, determined race, winning the *Observer* trophy overall in *Pen Duick IV*, taking 20 days 13 hours and 15 minutes. He also collected the multi-hull handicap trophy. Second came Jean-Yves Terlain in the huge aluminium staysail schooner *Vendredi XIII*, while in third place was Jean-Marie Vidal sailing *Cap 33*. Fourth home was Britisher Brian Cooke in *British Steel*. The winner of the mono-hull yachts (on corrected time) was Guy Hornett's *Blue Smoke*, whose time (uncorrected) was 36 days 21 hours and 26 minutes. In the under-35-footers the winner was Frenchman Alain Gliksman in *Toucan*, whose time was 28 days 12 hours and 54 minutes. American Tom Follett in *Three Cheers* collected the Ida Lewis trophy for the first American to finish.

It had been a memorable race and multi-hull enthusiasts, not to mention the French, had good reason to be pleased. Probably each successive trans-Atlantic solo race will see ever larger entries. At this rate the singlehander racing fraternity will perhaps come to outnumber the cruisers. Of course there are, and always will be, those who do both. It may be that the gap between the concepts is narrowing, at least in the middle regions, but where the purists are concerned the two concepts are poles apart. There is a vast divergence between the approach to singlehanded sailing of Moitessier and Tabarly.

Mention once again of Eric Tabarly can serve as a reminder that by no means all singlehanded solo ocean races are sailed across the Atlantic. In 1969 a singlehanded trans-Pacific race was organized by the Slocum Society of America, starting from San Francisco with the finishing line at the entrance to the Bay of Tokyo. Competing yachts had to be single-hulled and of an overall length between twenty-two and thirty-five feet.

Apart from the fact that the distance is greater there are other important differences between the Pacific and the Atlantic races. For example the starting date of the former, being earlier in the year, with winter barely past, means

Conversation between Dr David Lewis (left), one of the original five entrants in the 1960 Transatlantic race, and Jean Lacombe, the French entrant in 'Cap Horn', **a centreboard sloop**

that the competing boats are more liable to run into Westerly storms. Again, the latitude of both the starting and finishing lines is much further south in the case of the trans-Pacific race. The chief effect of this is that yachts have a shorter distance to sail in order to pick up the Trade Winds.

In 1969 the following experienced yachtsmen came to the line to enter for the Slocum Society's race. American Jerry Cartwright from Texas, with a new boat 35ft long, specially designed for the race; German Claus Hehner sailing a Tina yacht which had been shortened by a foot at the stern to bring her within the 35ft limit; Belgian René Hauwaert whose boat was a steel-built yawl. There were two French entries, Jean-Yves Terlain in sloop-rigged *Blue Arpège* and Eric Tabarly in *Pen Duick V*. Tabarly's boat, especially built, and with all his know-how behind the design, was also the maximum permitted overall length of 35ft. Like Terlain's craft, she was sloop-rigged and had as was to be expected a number of novel features such as a knuckle going all round the hull above the water-line, the purpose of which was to increase stability when heeled; also sea-water tanks at each side of the hull. This was to allow Tabarly to pump the weather tank full, again with the object of stability. As no restrictions had been placed on the draught of competing boats, *Pen Duick V* was given a fin and a bulb keel of 7ft 6in. Both keel and rudder (placed right aft) were at the same angle to the load water line when seen in profile. The narrow, deep keel carried a trim-tab on its after edge; the object of this is not to help the steering of the vessel, but by deflecting the tab a few degrees, and so giving the centre-line of the keel a curve, it increases the lift of the latter, a similar effect to the curve in an airplane's wing or the curve of a sail. The trim-tab was controlled from the cockpit. *Pen Duick V*'s displacement varied from 3.2 to 3.7 tons, according to the amount of water carried in the ballast tanks. To make the boat as light as possible, Tabarly had her built in aluminium alloy, a material which in his opinion is by far the best for yachts. The naval architects responsible were Michel Bigoin and Daniel Duvergie, and she was built by La Perrière, Lorient, France. The boat, as with all the singlehanders, was fitted with self-steering gear.

It was a fascinating race. Tabarly was first, taking 39 days 15 hours and 44 minutes; *Pen Duick V* had sailed 5700 miles at an average speed of six knots.

Although he sailed a shorter distance by about 100 miles, Jean-Yves Terlain took 50 days 10 hours and 43 minutes to come second. Tabarly crossed the finishing line on 24 April, and it was not until 5 May that Terlain's *Blue Arpège* did the same. Jean-Yves Terlain was well aware that the new *Pen Duick V* was the faster boat and he deliberately chose a route along the northern limit of the Trade Winds, so as to shorten his course as much as possible. The northerly route of Claus Hehner followed the Great Circle route, and by taking this and reducing the length of the ocean crossing Hehner deliberately risked bad weather. He did in fact meet some: strong headwinds up to fifty-eight knots forced him to alter course west and south to come down to latitude 40°. Hehner took 52 days 16 hours and 3 minutes over the crossing, arriving on 7 May to take third place.

René Hauwaert, sailing his ketch *Vent de Suroit*, took a more southerly route. He was, in fact, a whole month behind comparatively early in the race. He admitted freely that making the crossing, rather than winning, was his object, and his boat was no racer. Jerry Cartwright was unlucky enough to be hurled out of his bunk during a severe squall, hitting his head in the process. Consequent damage to his ear resulted in complete loss of balancing sense, and since this was accompanied by sickness it required considerable guts to get as far as Pearl Harbour, Hawaiian Islands. He was taken to hospital, and after examination lasting over some days was advised to retire from the race; a disappointing end to the challenge by this resourceful and courageous American singlehander.

Very different from the competitive-minded racing yachtsman and singlehander Eric Tabarly is fellow Frenchman Bernard Moitessier, since although he has competed in races he is a true solitary sailor, preferring to cruise the world's oceans untainted by such considerations as speed or a particular goal or destination. Romantic soloist, lover of the sea, superb seaman, author Moitessier typifying as he does the true singlehander would seem a most appropriate person with which to close this chapter.

What a remarkable band of men and women these singlehanders are! I think Joshua Slocum, first of the circumnavigators, spoke for them all when he said: 'To face the elements is, to be sure, no light matter when the sea is in its greatest mood. You must then know the sea, and know that you know it, and not forget that it was made to be sailed over.'

6

ANCIENT SKILLS

THE VIKINGS in the north, and the Mediterranean races who harnessed the wind to drive their ships in the dawn of sailing history, knew that from certain quarters winds could be expected to blow with reasonable regularity. They based their compasses upon them, the Mediterranean compass being boxed according to the prevailing winds in those regions and the Viking compass likewise. The seaman is lucky in that a constant system of both winds and currents exists, for it enables him to plan a passage with some degree of certainty. The sailor who uses the method of propulsion which gives him his name has to know and understand the winds, currents, streams and drifts of the world. This has always been so, and it is so for the singlehanded yachtsman.

The very fact that Chay Blyth's voyage (which went, in the southern latitudes, against the prevailing Westerlies) has been called the wrong way round, emphasizes this point. The fact that he was able to get round is a tribute to the man and to the windward sailing abilities of a modern ocean-cruiser-racer. If one can use the prevailing systems, it is obviously going to make life a lot easier.

Look if you will, at the charts on pages 130-3. Here the main wind systems of the world are shown in summer and winter. Winds may be classified as follows: permanent winds, for example the Trade Winds; prevailing winds, for example the Westerlies blowing between 30° and 60°, both north and south of the Equator; variable winds, such as those which blow between the Trade Winds and the Westerlies (see charts); seasonal winds, such as Monsoons and Diurnal winds, the off-and-on-shore breezes produced by local conditions.

If you inflate a balloon and then release it, the air leaving the high pressure inside the balloon will rapidly flow out to the relatively low pressure outside. The permanent and prevailing winds follow this law, the movement of air from a high pressure area to one of low pressure. (At risk of being accused of insulting the reader's intelligence, I would remind him or her that winds are called after the direction they blow *from*, not the direction they blow to. A Westerly comes from the west.) A short study of the chart will show how long voyages under sail may be planned from the point of view of winds.

But help comes also from the currents. Look at the chart

(Previous pages) **First man home in the famous Golden Globe round the world singlehanded non-stop race, Robin Knox-Johnston is seen here aboard** 'Suhaili', **with a well-reefed mainsail in heavy weather off Falmouth**

on pages 136-7 on which the world currents are shown. At first sight they appear much more complicated than the winds, but examination will show that they form a basic pattern of loops, turning clockwise in the northern hemisphere and anti-clockwise in the southern. Notice too that they correspond roughly with the wind system. This is natural enough, the effect of wind upon water being first to cause waves, but in practice very little of the wind's energy is transferred to the water in the form of a current. The currents do not flow in the same direction as the wind. The chart shows how the land masses of the earth interfere with and complicate the current pattern, except in the southern latitudes where the Westerlies blow, causing a continuous easterly set, since no land apart from Cape Horn, and Australasia to some extent, interferes with its relentless progress.

These surface currents are not fast-moving. Indeed, over most of the ocean they seldom exceed half a knot (nautical mile per hour). Some, however, are swifter, like the Gulf Stream which can flow at four or five knots. Fast flowing currents are usually those in deep water, like the Gulf Stream. In a given time, this tremendous current can move more than a thousand times the volume, by comparison, of the Mississippi. Readers familiar with the exploits of Thor Heyerdahl in both *Kon Tiki* and *Ra* will appreciate the use which can be made of winds and currents to cover thousands of miles of ocean. *Kon Tiki* sailed 4300 miles in 103 days.

Much research has been done in locating the deep as opposed to the surface currents which we have been considering, and today oceanographers know a great deal about the deep water circulation of the globe.

Another nautical aid to the sailor is that of the tidal stream. The moon, and to a lesser extent the sun, cause a regular vertical undulation of the ocean by gravitational attraction. This vertical movement, known as the tidal wave, is converted into a horizontal movement as the wave is affected by land masses. The tidal wave itself varies from place to place. At the head of the Bay of Funday between Nova Scotia and New Brunswick, the range of the tide between the lowest low water and highest high water can be as much as fifty feet, while less than a hundred miles along the coast it is only two or three feet. The horizontal movement is called a tidal stream, and as a ship nears the

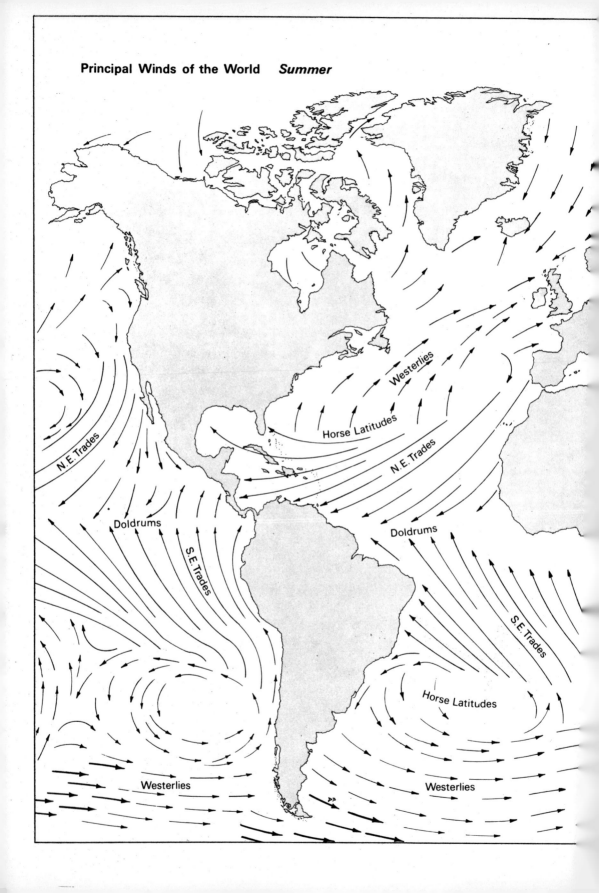

Principal Winds of the World   *Summer*

Westerlies

Horse Latitudes

N.E. Trades

N.E. Trades

Doldrums

Doldrums

S.E. Trades

S.E. Trades

Horse Latitudes

Westerlies

Westerlies

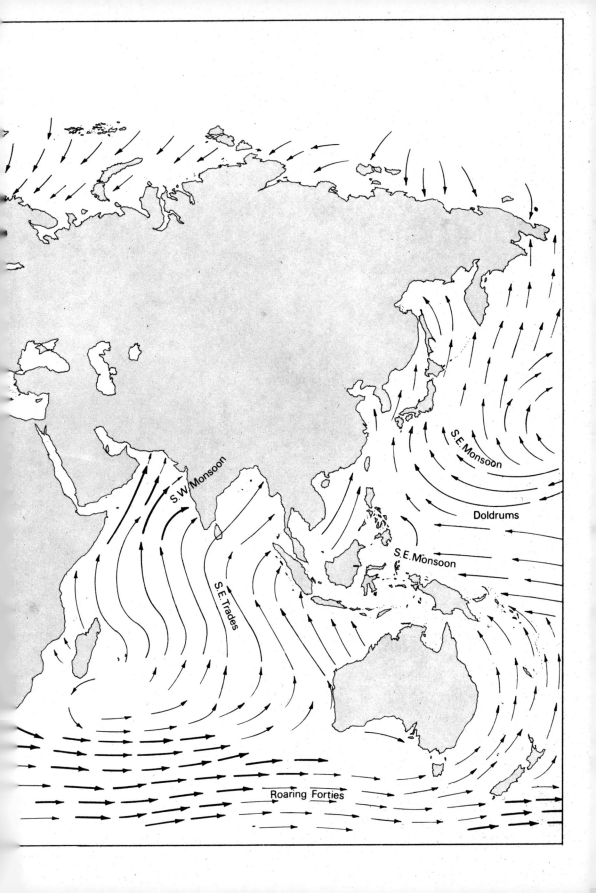

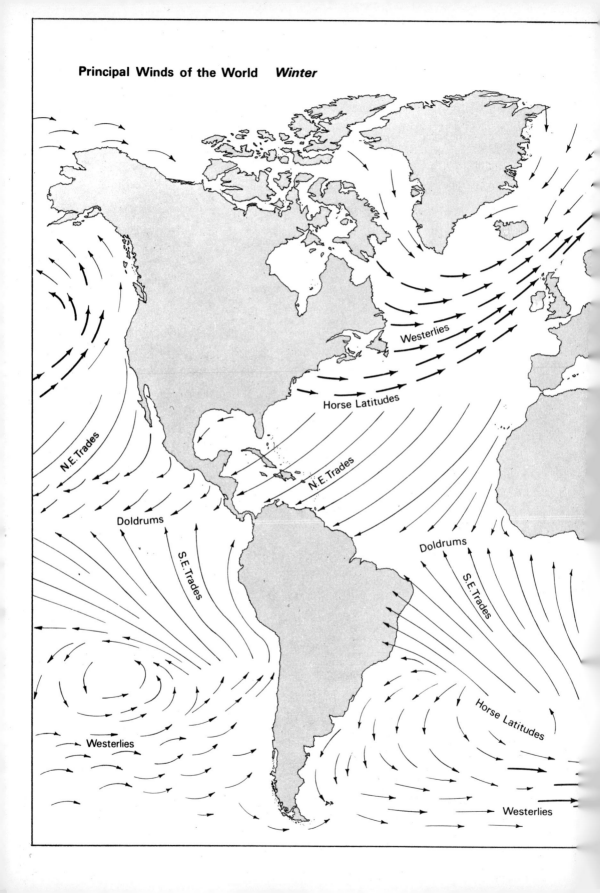

Principal Winds of the World *Winter*

Westerlies

Horse Latitudes

N.E. Trades

N.E. Trades

Doldrums

Doldrums

S.E. Trades

S.E. Trades

Westerlies

Horse Latitudes

Westerlies

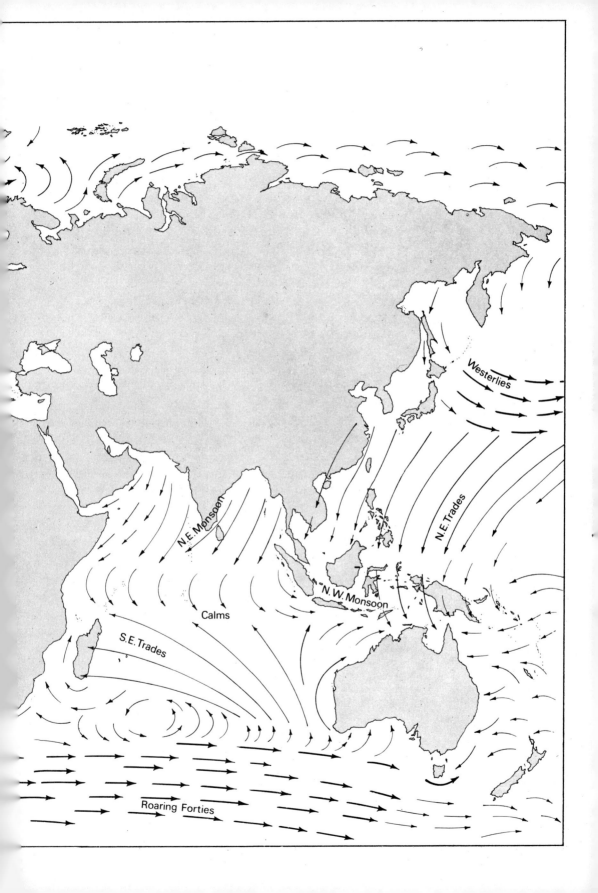

coast these streams play an important part in aiding or hindering her progress. The navigator must calculate the tidal stream's speed or rate and direction. He must also know the height of the tide, in other words the depth of water under his keel, so that he does not run aground or get wrecked on outlying shoals.

So we have three factors, the wind, the surface current or drift and the tidal stream, which have been used by sailors for thousands of years. The seaman's life was governed by them. And not only the seaman. In England for example, in the English Channel one can generally expect strong Westerly winds from October to December. From then through to early spring we may expect the cold Easterlies. In June and July calms and light airs abound, while August ushers in the South-Westerlies which bring rain from the Atlantic and spoil so many holidays!

Sailing yachts, even multihulls, move through the water at a relatively slow pace, especially considering the enormous distances which the ocean-voyaging singlehander must cover. Picture a small yacht, a monohull, about 25ft on the waterline. In such a vessel you could expect to average about five knots. A man walking at a fairly brisk pace moves at about three to three-and-a-half miles per hour. With the sauntering average pace of a sailing yacht in mind, let us consider some of the distances the ocean voyage covers. Look at any one of the world charts in this book. Starting from say Southampton in England, let us assume a passage to the West Indies—a simple Trade Wind route crossing of the North Atlantic Ocean. We might call in at the Canary Islands, a frequent stopping place on such a voyage. Even that relatively short hop means a sail of some 1800 miles, and that is only half-way to our destination in the West Indies. If, like the contestants in the singlehanded trans-Pacific race of 1969, we wanted to sail from San Francisco to Tokyo, the distance involved would be something in the region of 5700 miles. This was the approximate distance which the winner Eric Tabarly sailed, and in a fast racing boat, averaging six knots, it took him over thirty-nine days to do it! Almost six weeks at sea! And when it comes to sailing round the world the distances involved are such that the layman often finds it hard to visualize. Look at any chart showing the Pacific Ocean. In the Southern Pacific lie the groups of romantically-named islands like the Society Islands, Tahiti, Moorea and others.

If you run your eye from say Tahiti to Samoa, unless you have an enormous chart the distance will not seem so very great especially when compared with that between South America and Australasia. Yet from Tahiti to Samoa is more than 1000 miles. An intimidating amount of ocean has to be traversed if one is sailing around the world!

The yachtsman can tell the speed of his vessel by a number of means. He can tow behind him a length of line (75ft), which is turned by a finned rotator at its outboard end as the boat advances. The line turns a small instrument with a flywheel attached to the yacht's counter and the latter registers the mileage. The device is called a log. There are also plenty of modern versions of it: electronic, which register speed as well as distance.

But perhaps the safest way of telling your average speed is to note the time you take to sail from one fixed point to another, allow for any effect of tidal stream, current, drift etc., and there you are. The only problem is how, in the middle of, say, the Pacific Ocean, do you find a fixed point? This is where the science of navigation comes in. In the yachtsman-author Erskine Childers' wonderful book *The Riddle of the Sands,* the writer states at one point that he would earn the reader's disapproval, and justly so, if he were to enter into some lengthy piece of technical writing. I have always felt that Childers was secretly longing to earn that disapprobation but afraid of boring the reader. Yachting folk delight in long-winded arguments about tide rips and races, navigational expertise in the handling of sextants in the pursuit of the elusive star, and all kindred subjects.

However, I am well aware that this is not the book for a lengthy discussion of the mysteries of celestial navigation. Suffice to say here that with an instrument for measuring angles called a sextant, a ship's position may be found: the science of navigating by heavenly bodies being based on the theory that for practical purposes the sun and the stars are stationary, while the earth, moon and other planets move in known orbits at calculable speeds. The revolutions of the earth are also calculable; therefore at any given moment the sun or celestial body can only be in one place. If we draw a line from such a body to the earth's centre, it will pierce the globe at a specific place, giving us what may be called the geographical position of that body.

Should the reader wish to go further into the matter

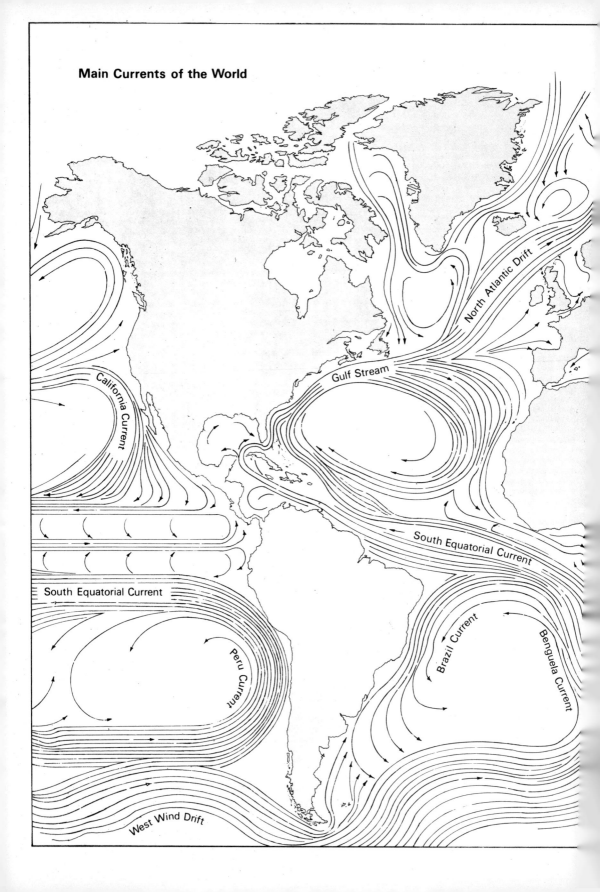

Main Currents of the World

California Current

Gulf Stream

North Atlantic Drift

South Equatorial Current

South Equatorial Current

Peru Current

Brazil Current

Benguela Current

West Wind Drift

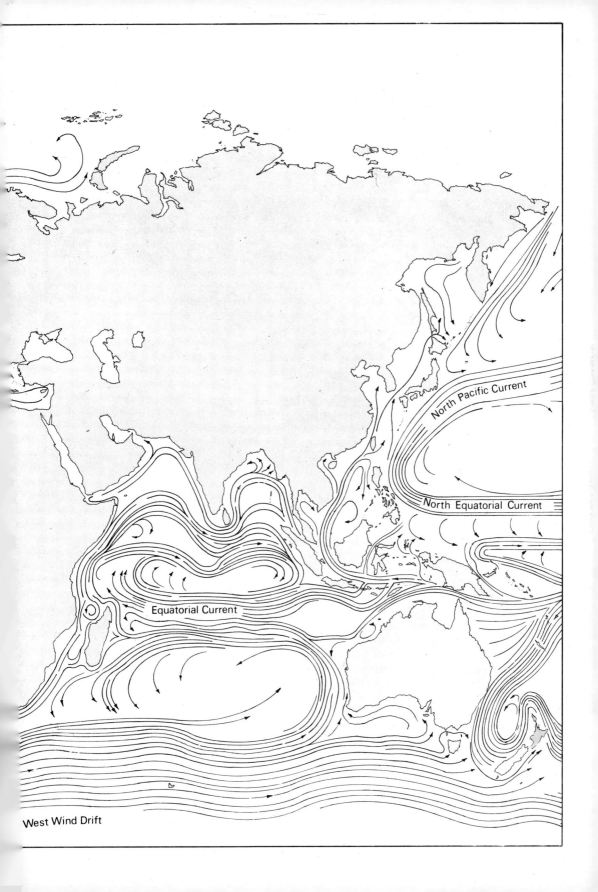

North Pacific Current

North Equatorial Current

Equatorial Current

West Wind Drift

From his ketch-rigged yacht 'Lively Lady', flaunting a rose on the vane of her self-steering gear, Sir Alec Rose, singlehanded world-girdler, comes ashore by a simple gang-plank

there are numerous excellent works devoted to celestial navigation, which is indeed a fascinating subject for those inclined that way. To any reader who finds my brief reference to the use of the sextant annoyingly tantalizing, I apologize, but I must stress that editorially it is outside my terms of reference here to satisfy him. If he should wish to combine the story of a singlehanded Atlantic crossing with a nice succinct bit of navigational theory, let him refer to Peter Woolass's *Stelda, George and I,* listed in the bibliography at the end of this book.

Using the winds and drifts and tidal streams of the world of water has long been the sailorman's art, and early voyagers like the Vikings were surprisingly accurate in their navigation. But if the safety of ship and crew depends upon an accurate knowledge of the former's position, so also does it depend upon the ability of the vessel to stand up to bad weather and of the skipper to handle that vessel. For as we have already seen in earlier chapters no long-distance voyage will escape its fair share of gales and high seas. As we have also discussed, the singlehander may be unfortunate enough to encounter freak conditions, huge waves, the result of a steady building-up of successive waves, and especially so if he be sailing the historic 'Clipper' route round the 'bottom' of the world skirting the three Capes: Horn, Leeuwin and Good Hope.

When winds of gale force beset a small boat there are various courses of action open. The following are listed by Sir Alec Rose: running before the gale; heaving-to; towing warps; lying to a sea anchor; lying a-hull. Let us examine these five methods.

Sir Alec Rose says he always tries to 'run' as long as he can, with the proviso that this is 'in the right direction', and reducing sail as necessary. He says that *Lively Lady* would not run under bare poles, and that in consequence he always kept a small staysail or storm jib set.

The principle of heaving-to is to haul the jib or staysail up to windward, leaving the reefed mainsail trimmed as if for sailing to windward. The boat, if running before the wind, has to be turned up into the wind, and consequently this must not be left too late. When a vessel is running before the wind, it is easy to underestimate its force, for the boat reduces the wind's speed by her own. When deciding to heave-to, the helmsman must choose carefully the moment when he turns up into the wind.

If the gale comes on to blow from windward then the helmsman will carry on, reducing sail by reefing until the boat is making such heavy weather of things that it becomes necessary to heave-to. Once the two sails have been trimmed in the manner described, the boat will lie quietly, but depending on her hull form. Some boats heave-to better than others, their general behaviour under such conditions being to range about, the bows coming up into the wind when the mainsail flaps; then the backed headsail pushes the bows off once more, and the mainsail fills and the whole procedure begins all over again.

Some yachtsmen recommend running before a gale while towing warps astern. Alec Rose always kept a rope coiled ready in the cockpit and lashed to the guard rail for this purpose, but he admits that no warps are long enough or big enough to stop a really big sea turning a yacht over. And Sir Alec confesses that on his famous circumnavigation that heavy rope coiled ready in the cockpit of *Lively Lady* was never streamed!

The sea anchor has long been a good controversial

For the third (1968) Transatlantic race, Eric Tabarly (seen here being hauled up the mast in a bosun's chair, with an anemometer in his left hand) entered the giant trimaran, 'Pen Duick IV'. But he ran into trouble, hitting a small freighter soon after the start

subject for yacht club bar argument, and I have heard much evidence for and against from people who have had personal experience in testing conditions. This anchor consists of a canvas bag open at both ends, one end smaller than the other so that it is conical in shape. It is, in fact, a drogue. The larger end is kept open by a metal ring or diagonal crossbars. But whatever has been, and will be, said on the subject, it cannot be denied that at the time of writing the sea anchor is out of fashion.

This brings us to the last method, lying a-hull, which in Sir Alec Rose's opinion is the safest. All sail is lowered and the boat is left to move with the sea, taking up her own position. Yachtsmen of my acquaintance have confessed to finding this extremely uncomfortable, an opinion which personally I endorse. But so much depends, once again, on the shape of the hull. *Lively Lady*, a traditional hull, lay in this fashion reasonably well, and Sir Alec Rose recalls how she would lie with a list to leeward keeping the wind forward of the beam. He admits that on occasion a sea would hit his boat with such force that she would be literally 'thrown about!'

One of the fascinating things about so many of the singlehanders' voyages is the way they kept going under gale conditions. This applies particularly to those who were racing, where time was precious. The dogged guts and determination of men like Sir Francis Chichester, Eric Tabarly and indeed all the singlehander racing fraternity compels deep respect. But sailormen of this quality will merely smile and remark that weathering gales, like navigating accurately by the sun and stars, is all in the day's work!

The modern singlehander has many benefits in the shape of aids to navigation, many of which, like radar, are electronic inventions of the Second World War. Varyingly sophisticated forms of radio beacon give assistance to the modern navigator, while the yachtsman far off-shore can still keep in touch by radio telephone. As he comes nearer the coast he can ascertain the depth of water at the flick of a switch from an echo-sounder (replacing the time-honoured lead line, which none the less every wise man has coiled below just in case!).

In other parts of this book I have mentioned the invaluable assistance given by self-steering devices, which can be set to keep the vessel sailing the desired course while

Sir Alec Rose's *Lively Lady*

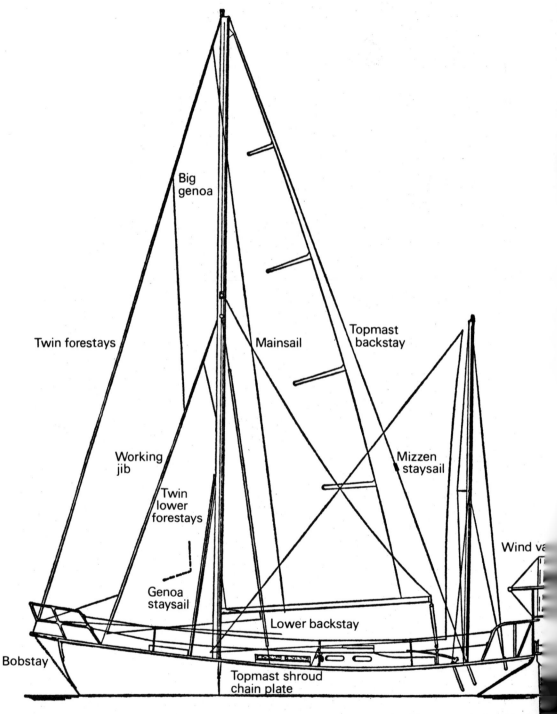

Big
genoa

Twin forestays

Mainsail

Topmast
backstay

Working
jib

Mizzen
staysail

Twin
lower
forestays

Genoa
staysail

Lower backstay

Wind va

Bobstay

Topmast shroud
chain plate

Servo blade

the singlehander is below, getting a meal or sleep. Such devices, like the Hasler-invented type of gear which Sir Francis Chichester fitted to *Gypsy Moth III* (and which he named '*Miranda*') have made possible the very long passages recently undertaken by singlehanders. It is perfectly feasible to sail across an ocean without self-steering; Slocum did it—and many others—but it does not need much imagination to picture what a boon this device, a simple version of which has so long been used on model yachts, can be.

Yet, enormously useful as all these devices are, it is in some ways reassuring that the man who would sail round the world must study, in order to utilize them to the full, the winds and currents of the world of water which have been blowing and running since the beginning of time.

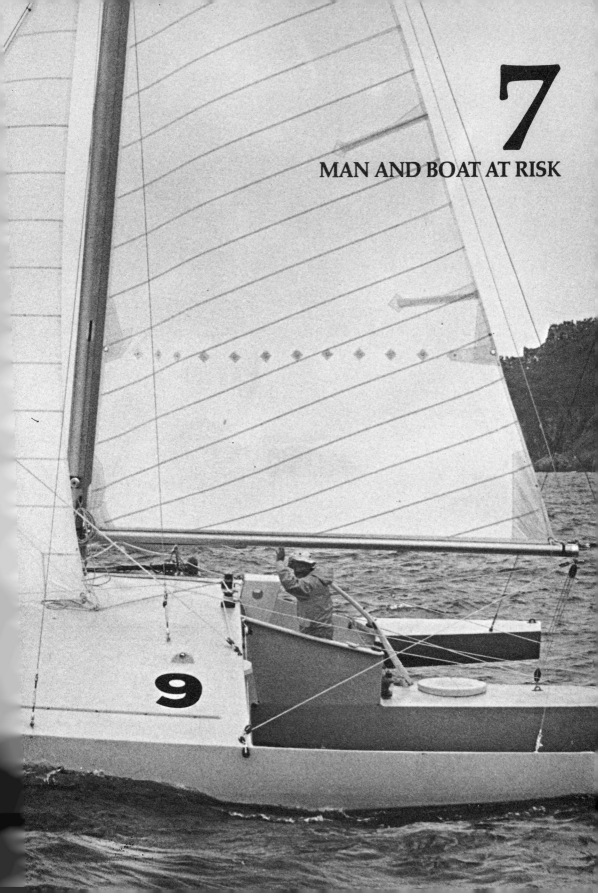

TO SAIL alone out of reach of help, into possibly dangerous conditions, needs courage. But what sort of danger does the average singlehander face? What is he likely to be up against? Lord Moran, in *The Anatomy of Courage,* wrote that there were four degrees of courage. There were those who felt no fear; those who felt it but did not show it; those who felt it, showed it but carried on; and finally those who felt it, showed it and, to use Moran's word, 'shirked'.

No-one is watching the singlehander. At the height of a gale he can do what he has to do, or—'shirk'. He is there of his own volition in the first place of course, and once at sea coping with possibly critical problems becomes a matter of plain necessity. Nevertheless some interesting questions are posed by this line of reasoning. Some yachtsmen have had relatively little experience of really bad weather before making a solo voyage, while to others bad weather has become less worrying through familiarity. Not all yachtsmen have made long passages without any qualms as to how they might react in storm conditions. Let us examine then what really bad weather can be like through the eyes of some who have been through it.

Take John Caldwell, for example. It was while he was sailing his yacht *Pagan* in that part of the Southern Pacific Ocean which lies north west of the Society Islands (a group best-known for the fact that it includes Tahiti), that he ran into a hurricane. The area is well-known for this type of tropical storm, which is a huge whirlwind round a central area of low barometric pressure. Caldwell was well aware that he might be unlucky enough to meet such a disturbance, but naturally hoped he would not.

On the morning of Thursday 5 September 1946, Caldwell woke to find a light breeze from the south west. At about nine o'clock the wind dropped, leaving a calm and humid atmosphere. Suddenly, a swell appeared from the north and by noon these swells had increased in length, making the boat roll uncomfortably. The swells grew in size and speed, one following the other menacingly in the steadily darkening sky.

Although relatively inexperienced, Caldwell knew enough to recognize the signs and he didn't like what they told him. But there was nothing he could do about it except prepare his ship for the coming storm, and this he proceeded to do. He battened down ports and hatches, lashed the boom and generally 'cleared the decks'. A life-jacket lay ready below on his bunk, and dangling from the bunk's side were a number of short lengths of rope so that he could tie himself in if things got violent. Having made everything as secure as he could, he returned to the cockpit and waited.

Visualize the scene. The Pacific Ocean is a vast area, in places incredibly deep. Shipping is relatively scarce today, but in 1946 it was much more scarce. If ever a man was entirely on his own John Caldwell was. He believed he had a good ship capable of riding out a storm, but with only an inch or less of planking between yourself and the sea, and with a hurricane on the way, a lot of faith is needed. Of course, to begin with Caldwell did not know for certain that it was a hurricane. For one thing, he had no barometer, which by its movements would have shown him what to expect. But one thing he did know—if it was a hurricane he was quite unable to avoid it.

With the evening and failing light came heavy rain and a strong wind that rose to gale force. A bad sign. There was no more doubt. Caldwell unlashed his rubber dinghy (his life-boat!) and pushed it off the deck, leaving it to bob about astern on the end of its line. As night fell the rain and wind continued, forming big, rolling seas, while in his small cabin John Caldwell lay in his bunk, looking up at the deckhead, and listened.

As he waited in the yacht's cabin Caldwell noticed gradual but definite changes in the vessel's movements. These became more violent, so that he had frequently to hold tightly to the sides of his bunk. He knew enough about the behaviour of hurricanes to be able to visualize what was coming. The wind had continued from the one direction for so long that it was clear that *Pagan* lay right in the storm's path. First she would be tested by the fury of the winds on the fringe, the semi-circle nearest to her. Then would follow the centre of the storm, an area of relative lull and variable winds, causing an appalling sea, and finally the other semi-circle of the storm in which, if he survived, sailing would slowly become possible again.

One of the most testing things about very bad weather is its duration. It can take what seems to be a very long time approaching: ever growing darker and noisier, while doubts about the vessel's ability to survive grow with the general crescendo of the storm. In such conditions a man can busy himself with making certain that he has done everything possible, and while busy he has less time to worry. But there comes a time when there is nothing more to be done.

By now Caldwell lay lashed into his bunk for hour after hour, snatching odd moments of sleep, and it was almost a relief when about 2 a.m. he heard a shroud snap and whine as it swished about in the gale. But the relief was shortlived as the mast was now in serious danger; conditions on deck were very difficult with a violently pitching boat, wind of a force he had not believed possible and a loose shroud whipping and flailing murderously—all in pitch darkness.

He tied a rope securely round his waist, made it fast to a handrail on the deckhouse and went forward to save his mast. In his book, called *Desperate Voyage*, Caldwell recounts how he managed to do this, only to lose the mast later while in the so-called lull at the centre of the hurricane, the airless sector around which the cyclonic winds revolve. It is a remarkable story of courage in the face of really violent seas. As Caldwell himself said, 'The process of riding out a hurricane in a small boat is terribly nerve-racking.'

It will be clear that John Caldwell, frightened though he may have been, was nevertheless reacting and behaving with courage. To be afraid is nothing: it is the way a man responds to fear that matters. Of course Caldwell was young and fit. Illness, it is well-known, can so increase the instinct for self-preservation as to turn a normally brave man into a coward. The natural resistance to fear can easily be lowered by almost any form of sickness and this includes sea-sickness. In his book Caldwell admits to the latter, and it is much to his credit that in spite of it he carried on with making such repairs as he could and pumping out the yacht which, after being dismasted, was half-full of the Pacific Ocean.

In considering the dangers involved in singlehanded sailing, the effect of fear must be included. Obviously no sane yachtsman takes on a long passage if he or she knows from the start that they are not only liable to be thoroughly frightened, but have serious doubts as to their ability to carry on under the sort of conditions likely to provoke such fear. Such a person need not be blamed. Private Angelo, in admitting cheerfully that he did not possess 'the gift of

Bank manager, Brian Cooke, aboard the 5½-ton sloop 'Opus', in which he gained a good sixth place in the 1968 Transatlantic. Cooke later sailed 'British Steel' into fourth place in the 1972 race. He is believed to have been drowned on a Transatlantic crossing in December 197

148

courage', put the matter into a generous perspective. Aristotle labelled fear 'out of proportion to the degree of danger' as morbid. But even morbid fear cannot be called cowardly. Cowardice is an action—or lack of action when action is needed. A man may feel like acting in a cowardly way, but if he does not do so, he is no coward. It is in connection with this that I have emphasized earlier the length of time for which bad weather at sea may endure, particularly the slow, steady, ominous building up of a storm.

It may be argued that the singlehander, being un-observed, may succeed in weathering a storm, despite having done none of the things he should have done to ensure the safety of himself and his boat. For relatively short passages, this could be true, but voyages of the kind we are discussing here bring not one storm, but many. There is the chance that successive gales may, especially if coupled with sickness of any sort, so lower the resistance to fear that the sailor loses, if only temporarily, his control. The instinct of self-preservation obliterates all else, and he cowers below as a man in a dream. It may be that while doing so urgent action is required on deck, and if it is not taken the chances are that tragedy will result.

This aspect of sailing must not be over-emphasized. The average yachtsman who takes part in an off-shore race lasting two or three days, will sooner or later meet bad weather. He knows this and does not give it a thought. The singlehander, outward bound on a journey across oceans, thinks, if he is honest with himself, a little differently. Exactly how he thinks will depend largely on how much experience of really bad weather has already come his way. In the tragic case of Donald Crowhurst, the man had lost his confidence before the *Sunday Times* 'Golden Globe' round-the-world race had even begun. Crowhurst is said to have spent the night before the race on shore with his wife, weeping in her arms, and although this was as much the result of nervous exhaustion as anything, yet clearly here was a man whose morbid fear was already beginning to get the better of him. Even an experienced sailorman like Robin Knox-Johnston (who had gained considerable experience in handling a yacht in bad weather when he brought *Suhaili* from Bombay to Cape Town, and from Cape Town non-stop to Gravesend in the London river) admits that at the start of his round-the-world venture (in the same *Suhaili*) he experienced the beginning of 'true loneliness', and in consequence had serious misgivings as to how he would be feeling after a week or two alone at sea if he felt so appallingly lonely at the very start. Even with his experience, on reaching the Southern Ocean (a part of the globe which Alec Rose had told him to 'watch out for!') he found himself wishing for the inevitable first gale to arrive so as to end the suspense. Although aware that there was no valid reason why the weather should immediately deteriorate south of latitude 40° south, Knox-Johnston admits that crossing this ill-omened parallel definitely had a psychological effect.

It turned out that his misgivings were well-founded. After two days of fair weather, *Suhaili* was 'knocked-down' by a large wave as Knox-Johnston lay asleep in his bunk. While working to clear up the mess down below, he noticed water coming into the cabin round the edges of the coaming, perceived cracks there, and further saw to his dismay that the huge wave had slightly moved the interior bulkheads. If the whole cabin-top should go, he would be in real peril. The thought made him feel literally sick in the pit of his stomach, as well it might! But the cabin didn't go, and as everyone knows Knox-Johnston survived not only that but many other gales.

Of course he not only knew about bad weather (having thirteen years' experience in the Merchant Navy in addition to sailing *Suhaili* back from Bombay), he was aware of the experiences of the first of the 'one stop only' singlehander circumnavigators, Sir Francis Chichester, who had suffered a severe knock-down in the Southern Ocean which he described graphically in his book about his voyage round the world.

Chichester may have avoided hurricanes but he could not escape the large waves likely to be found in the 'Roaring Forties'. The word hurricane applies mainly to the Caribbean and the South Pacific. In the Indian Ocean, the Australian seas and the bay of Bengal, these storms are called cyclones, while in the China seas they are known as typhoons. The winds revolve in a clockwise direction in the southern hemisphere and anti-clockwise in the northern, blowing in each case towards the centre of the storm in a spiral.

In a study of singlehanders it is misleading to emphasize hurricane risks too much. In the traditional route round

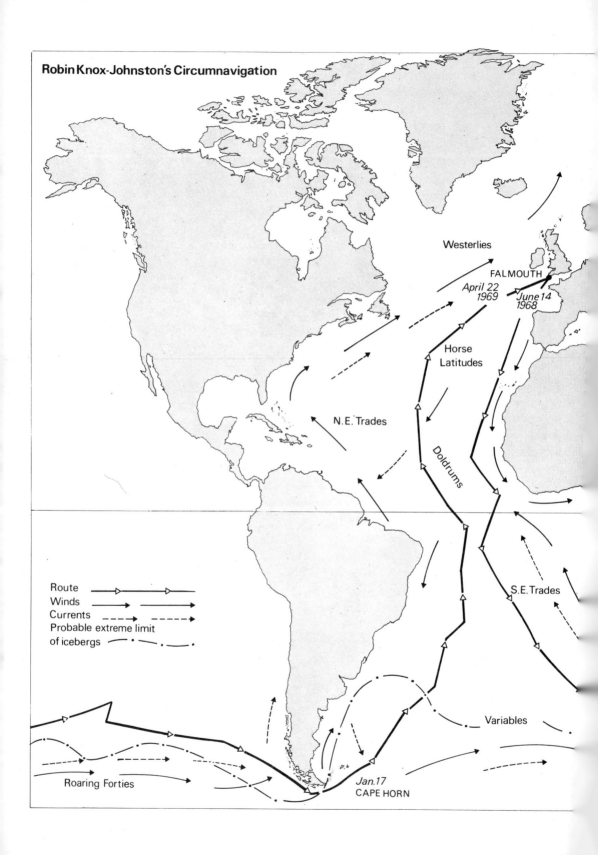

Robin Knox-Johnston's Circumnavigation

Westerlies

FALMOUTH
April 22 1969   *June 14 1968*

Horse Latitudes

N.E. Trades

Doldrums

S.E. Trades

Variables

Route

Winds

Currents

Probable extreme limit of icebergs

Roaring Forties

Jan. 17 CAPE HORN

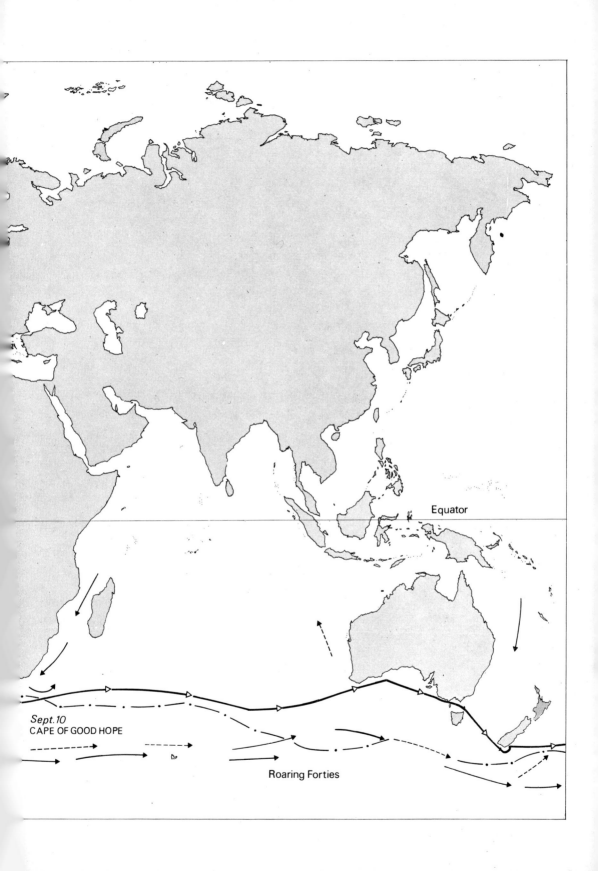

Equator

Sept. 10
CAPE OF GOOD HOPE

Roaring Forties

the world the vessel, keeping as she does in the region of latitude 40° south apart from the route up and down the Atlantic, does not in fact normally pass through hurricane areas. It is also possible to circumnavigate the world avoiding the worst conditions likely to be met within the 'Roaring Forties'. John Guzzwell's route in *Trekka* kept north of latitude 40° south, but when he shipped as crew with the Smeetons in *Tzu Hang* he experienced a freak wave well south of parallel forty!

Looking back on this event Guzzwell is of the opinion that any small yacht—less than fifty feet overall—could not avoid being knocked-down and capsized if unlucky enough to meet with one of the Southern Ocean's freak waves. The destructive power of such a wave is difficult to picture, but visualize the yacht, a two-masted vessel, sailing happily along; the wave building up astern of her, catching up and literally throwing her stern over bows; a complete somersault. Both masts were smashed into short lengths, and looked as if they had 'exploded apart'. The cabin doghouse had been sheared off clean at deck level, and the two dinghies had both disappeared. Yet the Smeetons, with John Guzzwell's help, succeeded in saving their boat and eventually reached the South American coast under makeshift rig. A remarkable enough feat, and they were three; imagine the same situation confronting a single-hander. Yet this happened to John Caldwell in *Pagan* when a big sea threw the boat right over until the 'beam planking became the deck'. He remembers the crack of solid timber as the mast went. And Caldwell too managed to save his ship. He truly showed courage, for he admits to being desperately afraid of this storm. When the gust that knocked down his boat first hit and the vessel heeled right to her beam ends, the timbers creaking so loudly that they could be heard above that fearful wind, Caldwell has said that 'in abject terror' he fled below to the cabin.

No-one is there on board to see how the singlehanded yachtsman reacts to violent weather and the deliberating effect of continuous gales. But in considering singlehanded sailing from the point of view of the inherent dangers and risks, it must be realized that while bad weather can be encountered almost anywhere, those who sail the furthest take the greater risk. This is in the nature of things. The North Atlantic Ocean is perfectly capable of testing the endurance of any singlehander who would cross it, but it will test him more if he makes his passage in winter—so he wisely does not. The circumnavigator endeavours to be rounding Cape Horn in the month of January or thereabouts, for that is the equivalent of high summer in the Northern Hemisphere. Even so, the circumnavigator who spends much time in the great Southern Ocean takes more risk than most.

It is however just a question of degree. The Atlantic Ocean can mete out severe punishment, as witness the experience of Frenchman Alain Gerbault, who, crossing it in *Firecrest*, saw a 'huge wave' approaching: a great, towering crested monster which broke on the ship, smothering her and hiding her from the view of Gerbault who with great presence of mind had climbed 'into the rigging'. In writing of this event and the damage done and of his efforts to make some repairs, he closes his description by saying that as it was growing dark and the gale appeared to be moderating somewhat he 'went below to get supper'.

This is the kind of calm resolve that wins the singlehander's battles. He may have no-one to observe him if he shirks, but neither has he anyone to share his burdens. There is no other person who by word or act can boost morale. In war a calm, offhand appearance of indifference when under fire on the part of one man can have an extraordinary effect upon others. The same applies to long distance (ocean) racing, when a determined skipper can keep his crew driving the boat at her fastest. The only skipper driving Sir Francis Chichester on his various singlehanded races was his own dogged willpower and determination.

But if courage is a vital part of the singlehander's equipment, one must be careful not to over-emphasize it. It is not my purpose to suggest that singlehander sailors are unique mortals, apart from the ordinary run of men. They are of course different in some degree, but they are usually balanced personalities well capable of self-management. While courage is an admirable thing, it must be combined with self-control and good judgement to be of real significance. In life generally there must be a balance between spontaneous action and self-management. Control of action without spontaneity results in a lifeless, rigid existence, but too little control and no direction just produces chaos. The balanced man is an efficient man and a sailor must, perhaps above all, be efficient.

In addition to being capsized by waves, a yacht can also be at the mercy of very large fish. Whales have overturned craft, and the small but deadly 30ft 'killer' whales have recently sunk a vessel in the South Pacific. In point of fact this occurrence, recounted vividly in Dougal Robertson's book *Survive the Savage Sea,* happened not to a singlehanded sailor but to a family. But it could have been a singlehander. These whales, capable of moving at well over thirty miles per hour, literally pierced the hull of the vessel in three places, resulting in an immediate sinking. The power of such whales is awesome. It has been suggested that the anti-fouling paint on the ship's bottom may have caused the latter to resemble a large fish, and this theory is lent credence by the fact that when the crew were in their liferaft after the sinking, the killer whales troubled them no further.

Steamships can also be a very real danger. The singlehander must sleep, for nothing produces faulty decisions and ill-executed evolutions better than extreme fatigue. The advent of the self-steering devices, which have facilitated long-distance solo voyaging, have also increased the risk of being run down at night by a steamer, just as automatic pilots on board the latter have also greatly added to this particular danger at sea.

The singlehander Peter Woolass, a Yorkshireman who sailed the small sloop *Stelda* across the Atlantic, has described in his excellent account of that crossing how when caught by a force 9 gale, he had to take in all sail. He passed an anxious night with little sleep, and with the coming of daylight realized how useful had been his electric mast-head light, swaying about in the sky and likely to be seen by passing steamers. In daylight all he had to rely on was his radar reflector, which was likely to prove useless in these conditions. Woolass reckoned any large steamer could run him down and 'not even notice it'.

Of course the danger of collision works both ways. The solo yachtsman may be below decks asleep and have the bad luck to sail into a small fishing boat. Such an encounter with a tough, modern yacht 50 or 60ft in length could result in sinking the fisherman!

The American Harry Pidgeon, who made two solo circumnavigations in the 1920s and 1930s in a yacht called *Islander,* which he built himself, recounts how he was sleeping below when he was woken sharply by the sound of the yacht striking something. Rushing on deck, he found a large steamer right alongside. He thought at first that the latter had run into him, but then saw that she was on the same course as the yacht. He tried to sail away and get clear, but was too close. *Islander* was trapped on the windward side of the steamer, and every large wave was washing her up and down the iron side of the big ship, even to the extent that *Islander's* mast 'speared' the steamship's bridge. Pidgeon saw a row of startled faces peering down at him; a rope was then thrown, and he realized that he was expected to desert *Islander* and climb up it. An excited and acrimonious conversation followed! At that moment a very large wave lifted the yacht to such an extent that Pidgeon thought he was going to board the steamer and take his yacht with him. For a second *Islander* was level with the steamer's rail, then the backwash from the latter threw her off and she came up into the wind and was able to get clear. He was not alongside more than five minutes, but as Pidgeon says 'it was the most thrilling five minutes of my voyage'.

It is only too easy for a yacht to get into trouble with a merchantman, as witness the sinking of a small cutter *Quickstep II* owned and sailed by yachtsman and nautical historian Frank Carr. It happened this way. Finding himself in bad trouble at sea, Carr accepted assistance from a tramp steamer, a Norwegian vessel of some 2500 tons which was in ballast, and consequently towered high out of the water. She had stopped and Carr took his boat alongside; a line came hurtling down from aloft and the small yacht was secured. One might be forgiven for thinking her troubles and that of her owner were over, but not a bit of it! The steamer was drifting broadside through the water and rolling heavily in the swell, and the suction round her bow and stern drew the yacht into her propellor aperture where she stuck 'like a stick across a sluice'. As each successive sea broke round the stern of the steamer the yacht rose and fell about ten feet. *Quickstep II* was doomed; held fast across the propellor aperture, she could not be shifted, and the tramp steamer could not be moved without her screw cutting into the yacht as soon as it started turning. Then a really big sea lifted her, and as she fell back she got the first direct blow from the steamer's propeller blade. With her port side cut in two from the garboard to the deck and with $3\frac{1}{2}$ tons of iron ballast on board, she

(Right) **It may look eccentric, but the junk (Chinese lugsail) rig is extremely efficient. And certainly were it not it wouldn't be the choice of original Transatlantic racer Colonel Blondie Hasler, a man of vast experience. 'Jester', seen here converted to this rig, entered for the 1972 race, but was not placed** (Far right) 'British Steel', **the elegant yacht in which Scots ex-paratrooper Chay Blyth made a remarkable solo circumnavigation, largely against prevailing winds and currents (often referred to as the wrong way round)**

disappeared almost at once, leaving Carr holding on for dear life to a rope ladder suspended from the steamer's deck while the waters of the North Sea closed round his legs. As *Quickstep II* sank she gave him a farewell handshake and marked him for life, for her topmast shroud, sliding down the rope ladder, caught his thumb as he clung there, tearing it off so that it hung by the muscle alone. He remembers only how the rope ladder was hauled up with him clinging to it as best he could, and he was 'dragged over the rail to safety'.

This kind of incident is not all that uncommon. Carr is an extremely competent sailor, but he was caught in circumstances beyond his control. Moreover, the incident occurred in the local British waters of the North Sea and not in the deep waters of the world's oceans on a long passage. It doesn't matter: trouble at sea can come in the first hour or after many months.

The modern yachtsman has much information to help him. There are known shipping routes, and the prevailing winds and currents of the world are known and charted. It is possible to determine where and in which months cyclonic storms are likely, and equally that certain areas are notable for lack of wind. But one thing is certain, and that is the unpredictability of the weather. No matter how much information he may have in the form of books and charts, and from instruments and radio-forecasts, the yachtsman is at the mercy of the elements. There will always be unexpected gales, freak waves, calms, fog and, in certain latitudes, that sinister companion of fog, the iceberg.

There is little doubt that the singlehanded yachtsman, whether racing or just making a long solo passage, who ventures unaided on the high seas is likely to meet with conditions which will certainly test him and may kill him by drowning. He may also be responsible for killing others. A singlehander cannot keep watch for twenty-four hours out of twenty-four, and as such he may be considered a menace to shipping.

If anyone invited difficult weather conditions it was Chay Blyth. As we have seen already he was circling the earth against the prevailing winds and currents, and one of the results was that instead of rounding Cape Horn later in the voyage this came in the earlier part. In point of fact he expected to see land on 21 December, and on the morning of that day he did so. The land was the high ground of

Staten Island, one of the islands in the Horn archipelago. The wind at this time was from the north and about force 6 in the Beaufort scale. Blyth recounts that there were cross-seas 'all over the place'. Navigation and handling were difficult and he admits to having no sleep that night. The barometer was falling all the time, an ominous sign. Blyth was also distracted by whales, about six of them, diving around and under *British Steel*. He recalls that he had small depth-charges handy to frighten them off if they tried to attack him; but they did not.

It was Christmas Eve when Blyth eventually rounded the Horn. In his log he admits to being very tired, having had only four hours sleep in the previous three days. It speaks volumes for his constitution and guts that his log reads so sensibly and calmly. Even so, he notes that the seas are now looking 'much more formidable'. He confesses, too, to feeling extremely depressed on Christmas Eve, and the loneliness of his position struck him anew.

(Time and time again one finds with the singlehanded sailor that it is some memory of a contact with the shore and friends and loved ones that, by disturbing the rhythm of their solitary way of life with the waves and fishes, by reminding them of land-bound things and people, causes a temporary but very powerful fit of depression.)

On Christmas Day the weather grew steadily worse, rising to a full gale, force 8, and force 9 in the gusts. The seas were becoming much larger, and Blyth notes about them that it was more than mere size but something particularly menacing that was new. One big sea smashed the self-steering gear beyond hope of repair, he was hurled across the cockpit and suffered a deep cut in his forehead.

The smashing of the self-steering gear was a bad blow. Like Robin Knox-Johnston, Chay Blyth now had to consider his voyage from the angle of doing the steering himself. No man can be at the helm all day and night long. He would be able to make the boat sail herself to some extent by lashing the helm and careful sail trimming, but doubtless he would have to stop periodically and heave-to in order to get essential rest and sleep. The only bright spots in the gloomy seascape at this time were the magnificent way *British Steel* was riding the enormous seas and the surprise of hearing his name mentioned on the Merchant Navy programmes with a request for the tune 'Moon River' by his wife Maureen and little daughter

Samantha. Even so that night, hove-to in the gale, he was unable to eat and found difficulty in keeping warm.

It is wrong to lay too much emphasis on the actual rounding of Cape Horn. Anywhere in the high southern latitudes, in which a substantial amount of the world-girdler's time is spent, can produce very bad conditions. Indeed one can meet with bad weather in any part of the world's oceans, and the risks attendant upon it are amongst the principal dangers that beset the singlehanded sailor, especially when fatigue is playing its part.

We may then list the principal risks run by the solo sailor as follows. First there are the dangers of being dismasted or, worse still, capsized. Then there are the mental hazards of solitude, bringing instability of mind and causing at best inefficiency. There is the danger of being run down by a steamer when resting or sleeping below, especially at night. There is the risk of attack from large fish or killer whales. There is the danger of illness, such as sudden appendicitis. The singlehander who makes no stops (or one) runs less risk of having his vessel damaged in port or, like Captain Joshua Slocum, being attacked. (Slocum kept prowlers off the deck at night by liberally sprinkling the latter with tin tacks!) There are other psychological risks. The singlehander can very easily acquire a taste for his pastime and can become so infected with wanderlust that if he has a family its harmony can be endangered. Having listed these risks, it is only fair to state that few of the singlehanders have succumbed to them. Nevertheless there have been casualties. Several have been dismasted and several capsized. Crowhurst, insofar as one can reasonably deduce from the evidence available, took his own life. Slocum is said to have been run down by a steamer at night.

To Slocum we are indebted for an authentic description of a freak wave. He was off the cost of Patagonia sailing alone in the *Spray,* when he saw 'a tremendous wave, the culmination, it seemed, of many waves' coming towards him and 'roaring as it came'. Quickly he lowered all sail and hoisted himself as high as he could in the rigging. Turning, he saw 'the mighty crest towering mast-head high above me. The mountain of water submerged my vessel . . . It may have been a minute that from my hold in the rigging I could see no part of the *Spray's* hull. Perhaps it was even less time than that, but it seemed a long while, for under great excitement one lives fast, and in a few seconds one may think a great deal of one's past life.' Slocum concludes by saying that the incident 'which filled me with fear, was only one more test of the *Spray's* worthiness. It reassured me against rude Cape Horn.' And Slocum's marvellous *Sailing Alone Around the World* has been reassuring sailing boat men ever since.

Of all the dangers the singlehanded sailor may encounter, probably the huge 'freak' wave is the most dramatic in its destructive force. Of course a man can be worn down by continuous very bad weather. As Robin Knox-Johnston said of the Southern Ocean: 'The frequency of the gales appalled me,'—but the sheer force of the huge wave is frightening. Although many singlehanders, including Knox-Johnston, found that towing warps astern was a help, Sir Alec Rose felt that the great seas of the Southern Ocean would take little notice and he points out that when Brigadier Smeeton's yacht *Tzu Hang* was turned stern over bows by a freak sea, she was towing sixty fathoms of heavy three-inch rope at the time!

If the worst happens, and the singlehander gets into such difficulties that he needs rescuing, he just might find himself in the waters of controversy. The Royal Navy and the Royal Air Force spent some £3000 rescuing Sir Francis Chichester in 1972, and questions were asked in the House of Commons about this use of public money. But while it would be foolish for any yachtsman to set out underprepared, and the main task of the military rescue forces is to help servicemen in difficulties, they can, in fact, benefit from the experience gained in rescuing civilians. Certainly, in Sir Francis's case, the Navy and Air Force were only too glad to come to his aid.

Solo circumnavigator, Ambrogio Fogar, first Italian to round the world, which he did making three stops en route, in his yacht 'Surprise'. Fogar is seen standing in the cockpit

ONE OF THE worst punishments which can be inflicted upon a man is solitary confinement. In such a situation the individual is completely deprived not only of human intercourse but of any novelty. Day follows day with appalling monotony. The majority of men find it hard to endure such isolation, which results not only in extremes of tedium but in an anxiety state, disturbed sleep and a blunting of the mental processes. Yet in effect the singlehander commits himself to a state of solitary confinement aboard a small, sea-borne prison for long periods of time.

'There's nothing like going to sea, for getting rid of all the poisons, you know.' These was among the last recorded spoken words of Donald Crowhurst, and sane and sound as the maxim would appear to be it was uttered by a man who, through the strains of acting a lie and of loneliness, was to suffer a complete mental collapse.

Donald Crowhurst was one of the competitors in the Golden Globe singlehanded non-stop race round the world, and while other competitors were in the act of circumnavigation, he had sailed slowly down the Atlantic Ocean, landed on the South American coast for repairs (which act disqualified him) then hovered about for a while in the latitude of the Falkland Islands. Afterwards he made his way slowly north so as to arrive within visual communication with the world at a time not inconsistent with having completed the course.

In setting out to win by deception, he had set himself an impossible task. It was a pretence which in reality he knew he could not maintain. Visualizing conversations with Sir Francis Chichester about conditions when rounding the Horn or the Cape of Good Hope, when he had done neither, was in his saner moments sufficient to accelerate his mental collapse. But he was a remarkable person, Crowhurst, and extremely painstaking when he wanted to be. For example, while sailing southwards off the coast of Brazil, he began making very full notes of shipping weather reports and continued to do so with the clear intention of building up a picture, of compiling an account of the weather in those parts of the world through which his imaginary circumnavigation would have passed. Not only the weather: he also made copious notes of shipping incidents, so that here, too, he would be able to lie

(Previous pages) **Donald Crowhurst's abandoned yacht** 'Teignmouth Electron'

effectively and hold his own with the other contestants.

Viewed in hindsight, it seems quite extraordinary that he should have thought he could ever have got away with it, and this draws attention to the fact that incidents throughout his life confirm his tendency to wild, ill-thought-out schemes, violent enthusiasms completely overriding all objections.

In carrying out his deception Crowhurst faced two principal difficulties. One was to avoid being seen by shipping or aircraft (since as time proceeded the difference between his true and faked positions grew ever larger); the other was that, being 'sponsored' from Britain, he was obliged to send his press agent, a man called Rodney Hallworth, regular (if possible) messages giving his position and general progress. Obviously this latter task was the harder. Perhaps I should not have written 'obviously', yet it is curious how very easy it is for a vessel to stay undetected for months in the South Atlantic, well away from the shipping lanes.

Crowhurst was skilled and knowledgeable in electro-technology. By careful wording of his messages and careful positioning when he sent them, he managed to get away with his lie. He was never found out, at least when alive, for it has been presumed that he committed suicide by drowning. This I must emphasize is not proven, but in a first-class reconstruction of his voyage, *The Strange Voyage of Donald Crowhurst,* by Nicholas Tomalin and Ron Hall, the authors' conclusion that no other explanation fits all the facts is very difficult to refute.

As his tragic voyage drew to its end, circumstances aggravated his problems. Crowhurst's boat was a trimaran, a three-hulled vessel, and in the race was another such craft sailed by Nigel Tetley. As the contestants neared Britain, it became clear—Moitessier having dropped out of the race intentionally—that Robin Knox-Johnston would be the first home. The winner, however would be the vessel which completed the course in the fastest time, and Crowhurst had started long after Knox-Johnston. As he came to realize that he might be emerging as the 'winner', Crowhurst fell back on the hope that Nigel Tetley would defeat him; to ensure this happening he dawdled on the homeward course in the Atlantic. Then fate dealt him a blow. Tetley's trimaran, already in trouble with leaks, broke up and sank. Crowhurst was now caught.

From this moment on Donald Crowhurst, as can be traced in the tape recordings and writings he left on board his boat, retreated into a world of his own. Sailing erratically up the Atlantic Ocean, he gave himself up to philosophical exploration. He had hit, he claimed, on the truth that he had reached so elevated a mental state that he was not only free of physical restraint, but could in the truest sense achieve salvation. He could liberate his own mind from his body, and could do so whenever he wanted.

Working out this theory of escape from the body, he wrote thousands of words—an extraordinary jumble of prophetic writings, scientific jargon and mathematics. It is a tragic and terrible picture: Hallworth's and Crowhurst's sponsors, including the town of Teignmouth (the yacht had been called *Teignmouth Electron* partly for the town and partly for Crowhurst's electronics business), and Crowhurst's wife and family, in England awaiting a hero, a victorious winner of the first-ever race of its kind; while up the North Atlantic sailed the object of their thoughts, going slowly but surely to his death. In all this, the man was desperately lonely; it may have been his own fault, but he had no one to turn to. Undoubtedly under such conditions the lonely life of the singlehander contributed to Crowhurst's death. If he had had a companion aboard it might all have been so different. People need to have a stable and reasonably good opinion of themselves, and they need the respect and esteem of others. These needs, true of all men, combine the wish for achievement and independence with the desire for prestige, appreciation and recognition. If self-esteem is achieved the result is self-confidence and capability generally; if not, feelings of weakness and inferiority result, which are liable to lead to the sort of compensatory trends we discussed briefly in Chapter 1. True self-esteem must be based on deserved respect from others, the word 'deserved' being of the greatest importance. Basing self-esteem on the undeserved opinions of others carries considerable danger.

It is not difficult to see how in Crowhurst neurotic trends built up as he lived his lie. To such a person loneliness and the solitude of the deep oceans, which the normally adjusted man of true self-esteem finds either soothing or at least lacking menace, become to the neurotic man something ominous, conducive of feelings of helplessness and threat.

But how far can the solitude, particularly of the huge Southern Ocean, affect a normal balanced man, if he has long periods with too little to do on board?

Sir Alec Rose denies that he ever felt 'lonely' on his great round-the-world voyage. I was 'alone but never lonely', he says. He admits to being frightened at times when, well out of reach of any help in the Southern Ocean, he met with conditions of vicious cold and gale force winds. But his fear was never, in his own words, 'extreme or paralysing'.

Sir Alec continually makes the point that there is always something to do at sea, therefore there is no time to be lonely, and the same emerges from the writings of Sir Francis Chichester. In his first account of a solo crossing of the Atlantic he recalls how after trying to reef his mainsail in extremely tough conditions of gale-force squalls, and finding it too hard, he had to lower the sail and hoist the trisail in its place, and then go below to find the Aladdin nicely warming the cabin and 'found that life is extremely good'. On asking himself why it was good, he concludes that this stemmed from the pleasure he derived from overcoming difficulties. Chichester never seems to have felt lonely. 'Alone', yes, and that he liked.

French singlehander Alain Colas, who circumnavigated the world in early 1974 in the trimaran *Manureva*, found that after passing Cape Horn in comparatively fine weather he had a period of about two days in what he describes as 'continuous funk' ('J' avais la frousse en permanence'), a real terror deep inside him. The region of the Horn, a region without human habitation, has affected many singlehanders from Slocum onwards with its aura of desolation. Colas strongly sensed its appalling loneliness, as he admits, and only when he had entered the South Atlantic did he regain his usual calm. Coming from a singlehander of proven toughness and ability this recognition of the corrosive power of loneliness at sea is of great value to those who would follow in his wake. Alain Colas maintains, though, that solitude is no very great problem on the whole. The fact of being physically alone did not worry him and he had always unbreakable links with his family and close friends to support him. He found a wonderful peace of mind: 'J'ai acquis une grande sérénité.'

However, the experienced ex-Merchant Navy man Robin Knox-Johnston did suffer from loneliness and its

problems. He associated it with boredom when there was 'nothing urgent to be done', and found himself 'longing for the voyage to be over'. Books were only a temporary palliative, and even cooking, which he quite enjoyed, became tedious. More serious still were periods of doubt. Knox-Johnston, in admitting such doubt, throws much helpful light on this question of loneliness at sea. For example, when he found himself getting into a prolonged state of anxiety and doubt he realized that the answer, for him at all events, lay in making himself do 'mental as well as physical work'.

He tried his hand at writing poetry, and wrote a detailed description of the self-steering gear which he had named 'the Admiral'. The difficulty often was that in very bad weather writing was only possible if he wedged himself in his bunk, and steadied the book in which he wrote with one hand. Music he liked, being particularly cheered by Gilbert and Sullivan, and his tape recorder was an acknowledged blessing. Not always the radio though! After listening to Laurenço Marques radio while in the Southern Atlantic he found it had a very depressing effect on him. Nevertheless he was still able to write in his log 'I do not allow myself to get maudlin over being alone.'

In 1971, a book was published called *Stelda, George and I,* being the account of a singlehanded trans-Atlantic crossing by Peter Woolass. In an interesting chapter Woolass confesses to some alarm at his mental condition during the early stages of his voyage. When darkness fell, he found himself below decks conversing with his brother and his daughter, who had been on board shortly before he set sail. He even found himself making tea for three! 'They really were there,' he admits, adding that it was the first and only time he had suffered hallucinations. He recounts how he fell asleep shortly after the tea party episode, and on waking and going up to the boat's cockpit was surprised to find nobody there. Checking his course he found that his self-steering gear (the 'George' of the title) had helmed a true course, and admits that he wept. Although he had no other hallucinatory experiences he did find that he was more 'emotional than usual' during the voyage, thus once again emphasizing the fact that for many people solitude creates anxiety states of greater or lesser degree according to the individual.

Of course Joshua Slocum, first of the circumnavigator-

(Above left) **Donald Crowhurst was forced by circumstances to put to sea in an unready vessel. He especially was unready and unprepared himself. Here, in some disarray, is the cabin of the abandoned** 'Teignmouth Electron'

(Below left) **Crowhurst, in his own way, exhibited courage in sailing** 'Teignmouth Electron' **to the top of the southern ocean. His is a curious story of an undertaking under insupportable pressures. The freighter** 'Picardy', **which towed the yacht in, looms over her in port in Santo Domingo**

singlehanders, had hallucinations, but it must be confessed that his were more nearly nightmares from eating over-ripe plums! Nevertheless the hallucinations were there all right, and the episode, recounted in *Sailing Alone Around the World,* is hilarious. Having dined too well off a 'white cheese' and the aforementioned plums, by night time Slocum was doubled up with cramps. A gale was blowing and increasing, and prudence dictated a reef. For what then happened let the captain tell in his own words:

> Plums seemed the most plentiful on the *Spray,* and these I ate without stint. I had also a Pico white cheese that General Manning, the American consul-general, had given me, which I supposed was to be eaten, and of this I partook with the plums. Alas! By night-time I was doubled up with cramps. The wind, which was already a smart breeze, was increasing somewhat, with a heavy sky to the sou'west. Reefs had been turned out, and I must turn them in again somehow. Between cramps I got the mainsail down, hauled out the earings as best as I could, and tied away point by point, in the double reef. There being sea-room, I should, in strict prudence, have made all snug and gone down at once to my cabin. I am a careful man at sea, but this night, in the coming storm, I swayed up my sails, which, reefed though they were, were still too much in such heavy weather; and I saw to it that the sheets were securely belayed. In a word, I should have laid to, but I did not. I gave her double-reefed mainsail and whole jib instead, and set her on her course. Then I went below, and threw myself upon the cabin floor in great pain. How long I lay there I could not tell, for I became delirious. When I came to, as I thought, from my swoon, I realized that the sloop was plunging into a heavy sea, and looking out of the companionway, to my amazement I saw a tall man at the helm. His rigid hand, grasping the spokes of the wheel, held them as in a vise. One may imagine my astonishment. His rig was that of a foreign sailor, and the large red cap he wore was cockbilled over his left ear, and all was set off with shaggy black whiskers. He would have been taken for a pirate in any part of the world. While I gazed upon his threatening aspect I forgot the storm, and wondered if he had come to cut my throat. This he seemed to divine. 'Senor,' said he, doffing his cap, 'I

have come to do you no harm.' And a smile, the faintest in the world, but still a smile played on his face, which seemed not unkind when he spoke. 'I have come to do you no harm. I have sailed free,' he said, 'but was never worse than a "contrabandista". 'I am one of Colombus's crew,' he continued. 'I am the pilot of the *Pinta* come to aid you. Lie quiet, senor captain,' he added, 'and I will guide your ship tonight. You have a "calentura", but you will be all right tomorrow.' I thought what a very devil he was to carry sail. Again, as if he read my mind, he exclaimed: 'Yonder is the *Pinta* ahead; we must overtake her. Give her sail; give her sail! *Vale, vale, muy vale!* Biting off a large quid of black twist, he said: 'You did wrong, captain, to mix cheese with plums. White cheese is never safe unless you know whence it comes. *Quien sabe,* it may have been from *leche de Capra* and becoming capricious—'

'Avast, there!' I cried. 'I have no mind for moralizing.'

I made shift to spread a mattress and lie on that instead of the hard floor, my eyes all the while fastened on my strange guest, who, remarking again that I would have 'only pains and *calentura*', chuckled as he chanted a wild song:

High are the waves, fierce, gleaming,
  High is the tempest roar!
High the sea-bird screaming!
  High the Azore!

I suppose I was now on the mend, for I was peevish, and complained: 'I detest your jingle. Your Azore should be at roost, and would have been were it a respectable bird!' I begged he would tie a rope-yarn on the rest of the song, if there was any more of it. I was still in agony. Great seas were boarding the *Spray*, but in my fevered brain I thought they were boats falling on deck, that careless draymen were throwing from wagons on the pier to which I imagined the *Spray* was now moored, and without fenders to breast her off. 'You'll smash your boats,' I called out again and again, as the seas crashed on the cabin over my head. 'You'll smash your boats, but you can't hurt the *Spray*, she is strong!' I cried.

I found, when my pains and 'calentura' had gone, that the deck, now as white as a shark's tooth from seas washing over it, had been swept of everything movable.

To my astonishment, I saw now at broad day that the *Spray* was still heading as I had left her, and was going like a race-horse. Columbus himself could not have held her more exactly on her course. The sloop had made ninety miles in the night through a rough sea. I felt grateful to the old pilot, but I marvelled some that he had not taken in the jib. The gale was moderating, and by noon the sun was shining. A meridian altitude and the distance on the patent log, which I always kept towing, told me that she had made a true course throughout the twenty-four hours. I was getting much better now, but was very weak, and did not turn out reefs that day or the night following, although the wind fell light; but I just put my wet clothes out in the sun when it was shining, and lying down there myself, fell asleep. Then who should visit me again but my old friend of the night before, this time, of course, in a dream. 'You did well last night to take my advice,' said he, 'and if you would, I should like to be with you often on the voyage, for the love of adventure alone.' Finishing what he had to say, he again doffed his cap and disappeared as mysteriously as he came, returning, I suppose, to the phantom *Pinta*. I awoke much refreshed, and with the feeling that I had been in the presence of a friend and a seaman of vast experience. I gathered up my clothes, which by this time were dry, then, by inspiration, I threw overboard all the plums in the vessel.

I make no apology for quoting this episode in full, not even to those who are already familiar with it, for surely it stands up well to a further telling.

Robin Knox-Johnston also had dreams, and he recalls how on waking he would remember that he had been dreaming about a person or persons whom he had completely forgotten for years. Most of his dreams were however about the voyage, but those in which long-forgotten friends reappeared made him wonder whether they should not be taken seriously. For the rest of the voyage he would 'recall forgotten characters and wonder'.

Robin Lee Graham, sailing *Dove,* admits that there were occasions when he wished a Slocum-type helmsman would come on board! Graham also freely admits that at times he talked to himself in a mumbling voice. He suffered greatly from loneliness and in his book warns off 'anyone who

hasn't first tried being alone for a few days', stating that some would 'return as raving lunatics'.

John Caldwell, after his grim experience with the hurricane that dismasted the yacht *Pagan,* had a series of nightmares. But they were about food, for at that particular time shortage of the latter was his main problem. He had managed to catch a fish, but was at a loss as to how to cook it. Then he remembered a jar of vaseline in the first-aid kit, and with this the fish was fried and eaten. The next day there were no bites at his fish line, and all he had to eat was the remaining vaseline in the jar. That night he dreamed of feasting and gorging'. The next day he mixed tooth powder with precious fresh water and drank it. But he came to bed 'unutterably hungry' and had the worst night of all: 'a succession of realistic food dreams, of chocolate cakes and steak dinners'. In this part of his fascinating account, John Caldwell recounts how he kept himself alive with the most bizarre and unlikely sustenance, ranging from lipstick and face cream to a small bird fried in engine

Followed by an asortment of craft, Frenchman Alain Colas is seen aboard his trimaran 'Manureva' in the bay of St Malo. Colas made a remarkable record-breaking, fast, solitary circumnavigation, taking only 168 days for the voyage

oil.

But when it comes to loneliness and fear Caldwell, whose account rings true in every line, is quite remarkably free from such worries. His main concern seems to have been that he should not fall overboard, fully realizing that should he do so he would drown. There was one time when he was genuinely scared, and this we have already touched upon in Chapter 1, when he was waiting for the hurricane to strike. On several occasions subsequently he was fighting for his life. But he was never 'unutterably' lonely; he was never fighting for his sanity.

Chay Blyth admits to feeling homesick on a number of occasions; suffering from fits of depression; filled with longing for his wife and daughter. Like other singlehanders, he was frequently depressed by gloomy weather, fog, rain etc., and when the fog lifted, he found in his depressed state that that the calm which followed 'was, if anything, more miserable than fog'. This part of his voyage in the early part of January in the South Pacific, having left the Horn, he found the most frustrating. In the calms in these high southern latitudes there is a huge swell. Blyth found himself swearing and cursing the place, and with characteristic good sense and humour devised a scheme of 'no swearing' with punishments for infringing the rules!

Blyth recalls how while in these waters his loneliness took the form of a sudden tremendous longing to be back at his home in Hawick, taking his wife and children for a walk. 'I wanted to get off the boat and *run* round the park.' An interesting relevation, which emphasizes the claustrophic effect of a small boat alone in the ocean.

Some singlehanders found that they felt particularly lonely in bad weather. In his book *Trekka Round the World* John Guzzwell writes: 'on 3 September I knew again the lonely feeling of a gale at sea.' Harry Pidgeon, in *Islander*, found the Doldrums particularly tiresome. At one point almost in desperation for something to do, he jumped overboard and went for a swim. On swimming a little way off to get a view of his boat he remarked how strange she looked: 'with all sails set', rising and falling, the yacht gave the illusion of 'gliding away' and 'I thought', said Pidgeon, 'how lonesome I would be if she went off and left me alone on the sea.' He had an impulse 'to rush to her side and climb on board,' although he knew the sky was windless. Eventually the monotony and loneliness were broken by the appearance of birds, like the man-of-war bird, and by 'an enormous turtle in the midst of a mass of sea weed'.

It was the appearance and behaviour of the creatures of the sea that kept Alec Rose from feeling lonely too. 'There was', he says, 'nothing to be lonely about when I heard a great deep-throated sound and I watched the graceful movement of a whale right alongside.' Dolphins were Alec Rose's special delight.

Paradoxically it is by no means certain that the innovation of efficient radio telephoning lessens loneliness, although at first sight this would seem to be so. By the same token loneliness would surely be relieved by the efficiency of modern radio sets, the ability of the singlehanderysten to music for example. Yet many of the singlehanders have said that when the conversation or the concert stops, and one is alone with the peculiar creaks, groans, swishes and small bumps of a boat at sea, the sense of loneliness, having been temporarily blotted out, is redoubled.

While in the southern latitudes Chay Blyth was stricken with chilblains and his feet began to hurt badly. He says he would never have believed that chilblains could hurt so much. And this brings me to the other subject of this chapter, the risk of illness at sea.

Anyone who goes to sea on even a relatively short passage has, if he or she is sensible, a first-aid kit or box on board and some knowledge of simple first aid. How much more essential, then, that the singlehanded long-distance sailor should know what to do in an emergency. That I have followed with this point so hard on the heels of the subject of radio telephone, is at least partly because, should a serious emergency occur, it is nowadays possible in many—although not in all—cases to summon help by its use.

It is remarkable, in point of fact, how few singlehanders have been seriously ill at sea, although one can of course quote cases. In the *Observer* sponsored singlehanded trans-Atlantic of 1972, for example, French entrant Yves Olivaux, a sixty-two-year-old former pilot of jet aircraft, finished the course in spite of suspected fractures of wrist and elbow from a fall on deck just after the start of the race. (In fact it turned out to be a severe strain of the wrist.) Another French competitor in the same race, Marc Linski, had to put his right hand in a splint and sail the last 1400 miles of the passage using only his left. Both men sailed in

considerable pain and showed great courage, and there have been numcrous similar examples over the past century.

Fractures and sprains are two of the more common and to-be-expected first-aid risks, among which I would list cramp, heat-stroke, sunburn and food poisoning. Such things as acute abdominal emergencies and asphyxia are more serious. There are some things which necessitate the presence of at least one other person, and where first aid is concerned, the singlehander is in a special predicament. There is also the serious problem of feverish illness. In a magnificent story called *The Cruise of the Teddy*, Erling Tambs recounts how he sailed the 40ft pilot boat *Teddy* from Oslo to the South Pacific Islands via the Panama Canal. Tambs sailed not alone, but with his wife and child and an Alsatian dog called 'Spare Provisions'. Yet during the passage an incident occurred humorous, yet with undertones of grimness, which underlines the impossibility of the singlehander's being able to deal with all emergencies at sea.

While in the Pacific, Erling Tambs contracted influenza and soon was running a high temperature. In addition, a poisoned right hand had begun to trouble him. Each succeeding day found him more feverish and progressively weaker. Tambs recounts how the doctor in Pago-Pago had replenished *Teddy*'s first-aid kit with a variety of medicines. Among these Tambs found some Epsom salts which he used freely both internally and externally, besides taking doses of quinine and aspirin to fight the fever. But nothing did him any good: while he was always drenched with perspiration, he was simultaneously shivering with cold. This, with the spreading infection in his arm, reduced him he admits to a 'miserable state'.

He now proceeds with admirable fortitude and foresight, to teach his wife not only the rudiments of navigation, but also how to bring the jib halliards down to the cabin, hook on to his body, hoist on deck and finally let go into the sea! The first few times the subject was broached his wife rammed her fingers in her ears and fled. But as Tambs' condition worsened and, in his own words, it seemed as if the 'Almighty owner of the *Teddy* might have it in his mind to discharge the skipper', his wife listened to his instructions.

Now they became not singlehanded, but 'no-handed'.

(Previous pages) **Chay Blyth waving from the afterdeck of** 'British Steel', **designed by Robert Clark and financed by the British Steel Corporation, the yacht in which he sailed 30,000 miles alone, to circumnavigate the world the wrong way round, non-stop**

180

Tambs' wife was fully occupied with the cares of attending her sick husband and their little boy—also sick—washing and airing clothes, cooking and doing countless chores. The vessel was left for nearly three weeks virtually to sail herself. Tambs writes the '*Teddy* . . . as though guided by a higher power . . . found her way.' Fortunately the weather was, and remained, fine. Erling Tambs did not die. If he had been a singlehander and had died, there would have been no one to bury him. But luck and courage were with him, and if he had been a singlehander they would probably have been with him too, as with so many singlehanded sailors!

It might well appear that of all the illnesses with which a sailor may be afflicted, and this includes sea-sickness, loneliness only becomes significant when for some reason or other, as we saw in the case of Donald Crowhurst, the mind is already troubled. Loneliness may be distressing but in the normal run of things is by no means incapacitating.

In conclusion I would suggest that in assessing what loneliness means to the singlehander we might do worse than look at the Concise Oxford Dictionary, where 'lonely' is shown to mean 'solitary, companionless, isolated, or unfrequented'; and that is all. Many people are lonely in the midst of crowds. To some the sort of loneliness you get at sea can be companionship.

9

LONELY HEROINES

Marie Claude Fauroux—attractive French entrant in the 1972 Transatlantic, who sailed a good race to finish in 14th place in 'Aloa VII'. **She thoroughly enjoyed the race but admitted that the 'constant rolling . . . made cooking a bit of a problem'**

ON 26 JULY 1971, having been at sea for 44½ days, a small 30ft yacht called *Aziz* arrived at fashionable Newport, Rhode Island, USA. At the helm was a small, dark, good-looking young woman who had just made history by being the first of her sex to cross the Atlantic Ocean non-stop and singlehanded. Her name was Nicolette Milnes-Walker. I say 'was' because she has since married and is now Mrs Coward. She set something of a fashion, for in the following year the 1972 *Observer* singlehanded Atlantic race saw three girl sailors come to the starting line: Marie Claude Fauroux and Anne Michailof of France, and Teresa Remiszewska of Poland.

The first woman to sail the Atlantic singlehanded, making calls en route, was Ann Davison who made her crossing in 1952. And in 1969, some seventeen years later, an American woman, Sharon Adams, chalked up another record for her sex by crossing the Pacific.

If we want to learn something of women's attitude to singlehanded sailing, therefore, we cannot do better than make a short study of these six remarkable ladies and allow them to speak for the many women who love to sail small boats. For whatever male chauvinists may feel about the matter, sailing—as anyone who lives near water where dinghy racing takes place can see—is no longer a male preserve. Neither, as can be convincingly demonstrated, is the singlehanded version of the sport. Let us begin with the remarkable Mrs Ann Davison.

In 1949 Ann Davison and her husband sailed from Fleetwood intending to cross the Atlantic to Cuba. Their boat, *Reliance,* was a big one, a 70ft ex-fisherman, ketch-rigged, and the intended voyage was in the nature of a move of desperation. A former commercial pilot, Ann's husband had fought a losing battle as a farmer trying to scratch a living from an island in a Scottish loch. Frank Davison had known many different jobs, being a Canadian lumberjack and gold prospector before joining his father's business in England as a broker. A keen racing motorist, he was also a pilot and it was the attraction of flying which made him leave broking to set up a small fleet of commercial aircraft. It was through flying that Ann, who was at the time working as a freelance pilot delivering aircraft, first met her future husband when she joined his commercial fleet in 1937. The Second World War put a stop to all private flying, and it was after several unsuccessful ventures, culminating in the farming fiasco, that the two Davisons took the decision to sell up, buy a boat and start afresh.

It was to be an unhappy choice. The purchase of the ex-fishing boat took most of their capital and fitting her out put them into the 'red'. The vessel had an old diesel engine on board, and much of the gear was awkward and heavy. Such a ship was far too big for the Davisons and for their pockets. The voyage, begun in desperation and ill-omened, was a disaster. A fire in the galley in mid-channel was only the beginning, though that was alarming enough. Their engine, which had all along been giving trouble, now faced a problem only soluble by making port, for it was running out of fuel. The Davisons tried to get to a French port but a gale blew up; the boat, far too large and heavy for their limited experience, was swept on up the channel into the race of dreaded reputation that runs off Portland Bill. The ketch was wrecked, Davison was drowned and Ann, incredibly, got ashore after hanging on to a raft in appalling conditions. The fact that 1952 found her sailing the Atlantic entirely alone, after the tragic experiences I have outlined, is why the term 'remarkable' is if anything inadequate.

Having survived the wreck Ann Davison set about earning the wherewithal to pay off the debts on the boat. In due course she was able to buy a new craft, but much smaller this time, a sloop 23ft in length called *Felicity Ann*, in which she left Plymouth in May 1952. Her voyage was not non-stop, and indeed she called in at several ports: Douarnenez, Vigo, Gibraltar, Casablanca and Las Palmas. She made the Atlantic crossing from the Canary Islands, arriving off Dominica in January 1953.

In an interesting book called *Last Voyage* Ann Davison related her experiences, and also told how she first came to sailing through being introduced to it by her husband, whose love of boats and the sea soon infected her. She has said that her Atlantic venture was undertaken to provide material for a book. Doubtless this is true, but there are other ways of getting copy and even to consider a solo Atlantic crossing after the ghastly experience of 1949 shows quite considerable courage. When one realizes that the woman who successfully brought off the adventure had relatively little sailing experience, the achievement is notable.

(Far left) **Mrs Ann Davison, whose tragic loss of her husband at sea and whose subsequent voyage alone across the Atlantic in 1952 is a story of adversity and triumph, is seen here in the bows of her 23ft sloop** 'Felicity Ann'

(Left) **A wave of farewell and encouragement to Ann Davison and** 'Felicity Ann' **at the start of her long voyage from Plymouth**

In my youth I remember fishermen who spoke of the sea as 'she' or 'her' and invested it with a personality capable of human emotions like anger when its (or should I say 'her') susceptibilities were offended by some disrespectful action. It all seems very far-fetched—to use a nautical phrase—today, yet in the exploit of Ann Davison I seem to detect a desire on her part to get even with the sea which had cost her so dear. It may be that by taking a small boat alone across the Atlantic, Mrs Davison felt that she had simultaneously fought a second fight as well as the one of handling a small boat in bad weather. Having triumphed, she may have felt (among the other emotions which small boat sailing induces) that she had laid a ghost.

Nineteen years afterwards another brave woman, Miss Nicolette Milnes-Walker as she then was, fought another battle with the Atlantic, and in so doing set up a record for her sex, becoming the first woman to cross the Atlantic singlehanded without making a stop. In the early part of 1971 she gave up her job as a research psychologist, looking frankly for adventure. She had always been an athletic girl, playing netball, lacrosse and cricket, and in 1966 she had become infected with the bug of sailing and added this to her accomplishments. This remarkable young woman is on record as having expressed the wish to visit the Antarctic, though not necessarily in a yacht. About her Atlantic crossing, she said that sailing alone was 'dreadfully boring'. Whatever she may feel about it now, there is no doubt that when she sailed her 30ft yacht *Aziz* into Newport, Rhode Island, on 26 July 1971, Nicolette Milnes-Walker had chalked up a far from 'boring' record.

Some seventeen years after Ann Davison's Atlantic crossing and two years before that of Nicolette Milnes-Walker, an American named Sharon Adams wrote a memorable chapter in the record of courageous women seafarers when she sailed her ketch *Sea Sharp* (may that be forgiven!) right across the huge expanse of the Pacific. She took seventy-five days to cross from Yokohama to San Diego in California, and in doing so beat the Japanese singlehander Kenichi Horie's passage of ninety-four days from Osaka to San Francisco in 1962. It must be recorded, however, to give a true picture, that Mrs Adams' boat measured 31ft as against Horie's boat of 19ft, and, speed being related to water-line length, clearly had a substantial advantage. Nevertheless, the thirty-nine-year-old American had made an historic crossing by any standards.

It was the result of careful planning. There is something typically American in the pains which Sharon Adams took to make herself expert in sail handling and generally experimenting, practising and studying her projected voyages in all aspects. She typifies the American will-to-win, so frequently productive in success in Olympic athletes, to say nothing of their apparent invincibility in the America's Cup races. She was fortunate in that her husband ran a sailing school in California, where for several years she was able to train. In 1965 came the test of a singlehanded passage from California to Hawaii, a distance of 2225 miles, taking thirty-nine days from port to port.

(Top left) **A great passage by a great lady sailor. Californian housewife, Sharon Tate Adams, sailed her ketch 'Sea Sharp II', pictured here, across the Pacific singlehanded**

(Below left) **Lively Nicolette Milnes-Walker (now Mrs Coward) aboard the 30ft sloop 'Aziz'. She was the first woman to cross the Atlantic non-stop**

When the time came for her Pacific adventure, Sharon Adams was well versed in seamanship and had the confidence which only comes from singlehanded experience at sea in deep-water conditions. Her epic voyage proved the value of training and her own fine qualities of courage and endurance. It also proved that marriage need be no bar to long singlehanded passage-making for ladies; neither need children, for Mrs Sharon Adams has two.

The two French girls mentioned earlier, Marie-Claude Fauroux and Anne Michailof, who took part in the 1972 *Observer* singlehanded Atlantic race, were to finish respectively in fourteenth and fortieth place. The Polish girl Teresa Remiszewska finished thirty-eighth in the same race, sailing the 42ft yawl *Komodor*. Forty-three years old with a son at university, Teresa was a determined sailor whose avowed ambition even at the time of the race was to circumnavigate the globe singlehanded and be the first woman to do so. The yacht *Komodor* was sponsored by the Polish Navy. Teresa Remiszewska, who comes from Gdynia, is a notable woman sailor.

Anne Michailof's boat was called *P.S.* A 30·6ft sloop, her real name was *Pieter Stuyvesant* after the cigarette company who sponsored her. However, the Royal Western Yacht Club decreed that under the sponsorship rule, recently introduced, to use the full name was disallowed. Anne was to be the last of the French sailors of both sexes to cross the line, *P.S.* proving to be a relatively slow mover. Under her time penalty she came to be placed last of the forty yachts which finished the course inside the time limit. All things considered she did very well.

The other French girl, Marie-Claude Fauroux, sailed a class boat called *Aloa VII,* entered in the race by the builders S.E.B. Marine of France. Marie-Claude was the most outwardly confident of the lady sailors in the race. A good-looking girl, she had been a 'Moth' dinghy champion and was convinced of her ability to be in at the finish with the hardiest of the men. She succeeded in winning the trophy for the first woman to finish but, as already recounted elsewhere, had no wish to repeat the venture. She wanted to prove she could do it—that was all. There seemed little point in proving it twice. She admitted to being afraid once when she seemed to be very close to the big liner *France,* but, all in all, seems to have had few problems.

This underlines what is perhaps one of the most notable features of these lady singlehanders—absence of fuss.

10
'SEAWEED' WIDOWS

Three wives, (left to right) **Mrs Bernard Moitessier, Mrs Nigel Tetley and Mrs Donald Crowhurst, meet on board** 'Discovery', **on the river Thames, while their husbands take part in the 1969** *Sunday Times* **Golden Globe race**

CHAY BLYTH, referring to the fact of leaving his wife Maureen and young daughter for almost a year asked 'Was I selfish?' Answering himself, 'Yes,' he adds that there must be some element of selfishness in any form of self-fulfilment. Maureen, he said, understood this and in this lay her 'greatness'. 'Of course there were times when I was anxious'; so speaks Sir Alec Rose's wife Dorothy, and no-one could have given more support to a lone circumnavigator. And yet—perhaps Sheila Chichester takes pride of place, for not only did she back Sir Francis to the hilt and encourage him to go on the first trans-Atlantic solo race, but she did so in the face of much criticism because Chichester at the time was thought to be still a very sick man. Time proved her right, but in all Sir Francis Chichester's subsequent races, culminating in his round-the-world marathon, his wife was to give him the same support.

The sunny side of the picture? Are there not really many 'seaweed' widows who are suspicious of the undertaking, resentful of being left behind, and even jealous? Some yachting husbands, reading of the wives of three single-handers mentioned, might be tempted to feel that Blyth, Rose and Chichester were unusually fortunate. For it is a fact that some wives are resentful of sports like sailing, which if they themselves do not participate, tend to take their husbands away into an alien world, sometimes for quite long periods.

The remedy often lies in the wife learning to enjoy (sometimes pretending to enjoy!) this curious pastime of being bumped about uncomfortably in cramped quarters frequently cold and often wet through.

Men are more often than not to blame for the dislike of sailing which some women feel. 'The only difference between staying at home and going sailing is that at home slaving at the cooker is doing it in more comfortable conditions,' remarks Mrs X, a yachtswoman of considerable experience, who insists upon anonymity, and there are many, to my certain knowledge, who would agree.

But the sacrifice is made, and the wife does 'go sailing' be it cruising or racing or a mixture of both. Dramamine and willpower surmount sea-sickness. She acquires a good working knowledge of boat handling and the salty jargon so often thought essential, and may even have progressed to taking star sights with a sextant, when suddenly her husband announces his intention to go off in the boat quite alone, for months and months on end, in the pursuit of something called self-fulfilment! No wonder Chay Blyth and Alec Rose value their partners so highly. For by no means every woman would understand.

There is also another very important side to the question, and that is worry. On one occasion, when Sir Francis Chichester was approaching Australia in *Gypsy Moth IV* in 1966, Donald Crowhurst had told his fortune at a party with a pack of Tarot cards. When card succeeded card, each predicting disaster and death, Clare Crowhurst became very upset. Of course wives at home get worried. Lady Rose says that she could not help worrying, but she tried to keep herself busy. She also said that she knew that if she did 'It would spoil Alec's adventure and make him worry too.' What an admirably unselfish attitude.

But there is the reverse of the coin. Sailors have long been accused of having 'a wife in every port'; less has been said about the actions of their wives when they are on the high seas. Sometimes a ship has had to put back to the port from which she had recently departed, and a sailor rushing home can surprise his wife, who might have a rival for her charms hiding in terror in a cupboard, as happened to David Niven and was recounted in his extraordinarily funny autobiography *The Moon is a Balloon*. The sad story of Morell in *The Cruel Sea* is alas based, like everything else in that book, upon solid fact. Such incidents do occur, and sufficiently often, surely, for there to be an occasional twinge of disquiet about the 'little woman' on shore? Especially if she is pretty and attractive.

Yet is this ever mentioned in the sagas of the singlehanders? I venture to say, never! Are sailors so conceited, or do they think that to pen such thoughts would be disloyal? Lady Rose was busy; she had a shop to run and that *does* mean busy! Can we find, however, any woman who does admit to feelings of resentment at being left? Not, it would appear, in the pages of the singlehanders' autobiographies.

But the following bona-fide conversation may be of interest. (The lady wishes to remain anonymous—for obvious reasons.)

Question: You have accustomed yourself to liking sailing

Lady Rose with Sir Alec aboard 'Lively Lady' when the yacht was on display at Holborn Circus, London. The statue of Prince Albert in the foreground appears very properly to be raising his hat to them both. Sir Alec is loud in his appreciation of the help and support his wife gave him

LIVELY LADY

(Far left) **Aboard 'Suhaili' in the London River, with Tower Bridge in the background, world circumnavigator and race victor Robin Knox-Johnston stands with one arm round his mother. Watching on the quayside is his father**
(Left) **Robin Knox-Johnston, winner of the Golden Globe non-stop singlehanded race round the world, the first man to achieve such a record, is seen here surrounded by his voyage provisions on the quay alongside his boat**

almost entirely because it is your husband's passion. If he announced to-morrow that he intended to go off in your boat for a singlehanded cruise lasting from six to nine months, leaving you and your small daughter all alone, would you try and dissuade him?

Answer: No. But I would pray that he would change his mind.

Question: Assuming that he did not, would you be at all resentful?

Answer: Not when things were going well at home. But if they were going badly I would resent it like hell!

Question: Would you expect him ever to worry about your being unfaithful to him?

Answer: Definitely! All the time! No matter how much you love somebody there is always the risk.

Question: I know you have read books by singlehanders. Why is it no mention of this question of fidelity is ever made.

Answer: I think because the books are written from such a very male point of view.

Question: Would you be worried at all about the risks of bad weather etc?

Answer: Yes, all the time; especially at night.

Question: When your husband returned, would you expect to find things strange to begin with?

Answer: I think my daughter would find it strange. I myself, perhaps, but only for about a fortnight, I think.

Question: Do you think it a selfish action on the part of your husband?

Answer: Yes. But I don't mind that. If you really love someone you must let them do what they want in this sort of self-fulfilment way, otherwise they will resent you.

Question: Do you know any yachtsmen who leave their wives behind when they sail?

Answer: I know one, and the moment he leaves the house on a long trip another man pops in the front door. Everybody knows about it. It is a standing joke!

Question: Do you like yachts?

Answer: No. Not particularly that is. I think men get sort of romantic about yachts.

Question: Is that a cause for jealousy on the part of the wife?

Answer: Good Heavens no! If it was, there would be something wrong with the marriage.

So there it is. Refreshing and illuminating. I may add that the lady in question is young and pretty and extremely capable.

There is, however, one aspect we have not so far touched upon, and that is the question of how far is it necessary for a singlehander to have a landbound partner? There is no doubt that support for this would be enormous if the question were to be generally put. And if the partner is gifted with the ability fully to share in the success of her husband, the pleasure is doubled for both of them. 'The whole thing has been a fairy story with a happy ending. I cannot say more.' So said Lady Rose; and it says so much.

It may not be generally realized, too, that the wife back on shore has quite a lot to do in connection with a big solo enterprise. There may be the question of running not only a home but also a business, or at least keeping track of things. And prior to sailing there is the monumental business of provisioning the boat. Chay Blyth wrote how much he owed his wife Maureen in this respect. She was working as a telephonist, and while on holiday in Newcastle she made lists of all the food which Chay would need on his circumnavigation. Her diary for July records how she not only helped with such important matters as sorting out existing charts and organizing the supply of others, but was a constant source of encouragement. On 7 August she was to write in her diary: 'I gave up my job. Now real work on trip begins.'

When Blyth read this he said that his first reaction was one of admiration for Maureen's loyalty, and when he realized what he was asking of her. He was doing what he felt he had to do and Maureen was backing him all the way. But from her point of view she had been steadily giving up the very things that make a woman feel secure.

Her work increased now as her diary had predicted, taking her one day to London to see about a compass with Chay and another to Southampton for a sextant to be checked. It was in September that she started making up what she called 'special day' parcels, to be opened on days of some significance on the voyage. For example, in Chay's 'Cape Horn' parcel there was a tin of pâté, a tin of potatoes, a tin of mandarin oranges, a game of puzzles and a cake made by the wife of a friend, Eric Lee.

It was not all easy going either. On 5 September Maureen wrote: 'Chay very downhearted. Everything not going too well. Still an awful lot to do on boat.' Blyth has said that reading his wife's diary brings a lump to his throat, making him feel selfish. He says that he now realizes he must have come near to straining even her wonderful loyalty. But she did not crack and Blyth wrote that he thanked God for her.

This epitomizes the perfect partnership, even if it seems a bit one-sided. The trouble is that so often the singlehanded sailing bug will not let the patient recover; after a spell of marital bliss on shore, he is often itching to go again. In his great film about the Royal Navy, *In Which We Serve*, Noel Coward made the wife of the Destroyer Captain say, when she is proposing a toast, that she will toast the ship. Celia Johnson, in the part, made a moving little speech in which she drank to her husband's ship, HMS *Torrin*, with affection because she knew how he felt about it, but also with the underlying fear of an undefeatable rival. Writers, playwrights and poets have for centuries been spinning a good deal of romantic yarn when the subject of the sea is concerned, and those writers about the sea who emphasize the romance of the sailor's life are not as a rule popular with women. The blue-eyed far-away look in the sailor's eye, yes indeed! The gallant fellow

A happy family party in fine weather—Sir Francis, Lady Chichester, and their son Giles. Lady Chichester was a tremendous encouragement to her husband

returning home to his sweetheart for an orgy of reconciliation, certainly! But when the same fellow feels 'the call of the running tide', and wants to be again as one with the gulls and fishes, the helpmate's smile can change rapidly to that inverted line which, coupled with an uncompromising stare, means, 'If you want an excuse to go off in that boat and leave me for another three months, it had better be something a damn sight more cogent than a quotation from John Masefield!'

Generally speaking, the wife of the singlehanded sailor goes along with it because she loves her husband, and if that husband overplays his hand who can blame the wife for feeling annoyed? It is one thing for Noel Coward to make the Captain's wife refer to her 'rival' in a wardroom toast, but quite another when the rival is a yacht, in time of peace, and when the absence not only runs into months on end but is liable to be repeated when the sea bug bites again.

All this would seem to prove that the singlehanders seem to get themselves married to some pretty wonderful women. In *The Anatomy of Melancholy* Burton asked 'What is a ship but a prison?' While accepting that the modern yachtsman's lot is not that of Jack Tar of pressgang days, yet for a man to desert his wife for even a modernized welfare state prison, and moreover a prison dignified with the pronoun 'she', is a double insult that only a woman is strong enough to bear with equanimity. And sometimes the joke ceases to be, and the story becomes stark tragedy for the waiting wife. It was on the evening of 10 July that Clare Crowhurst first heard the dreadful news that her husband's boat, *Teignmouth Electron*, had been found at sea with no-one on board. That night she refused to make any statement to the press except that she was convinced that her husband was still alive. Clare Crowhurst was Irish, from Killarney, very Celtic, and convinced that she would have sensed it if Donald had died.

At the time stories abounded that Crowhurst had somehow escaped to South America, although the evidence was strongly against any such possibility. The mystery was eventually cleared up, in so far as it could be, when his log books were examined, but one can imagine the agony and misery of the intervening period for his wife. When at last she became hardened to the fact that her husband must be presumed dead, she settled down to life alone with her children.

The sea in Clare Crowhurst's case had truly made a widow. It was a dreadful story, and one likely to stick in the mind of many another woman whose man was bent on this curious yet somehow gallant way of proving something to himself.

BIBLIOGRAPHY

Allcard, Edward *Singlehanded Passage* Putnam 1950; Norton
    1950 *Temptress Returns* Putnam 1952; Norton 1953
    Voyage Alone Hale 1967; Dodd, Mead of Canada 1964

Blythe, Chay *Impossible Voyage* Hodder & Stoughton 1971;
    Putnam 1972

Caldwell, John *Desperate Voyage* Gollancz 1950; Little, Brown
    1949

Chichester, Francis *Atlantic Adventure* Allen & Unwin 1962
    Alone Across the Atlantic Allen & Unwin 1968; Doubleday
    1963 *The Lonely Sea and the Sky* Hodder & Stoughton
    1964; Ballantine 1971

Childers, Erskine *The Riddle of the Sands* Hart-Davis 1968;
    Dutton 1970

Davison, Ann *Last Voyage* Peter Davies 1951; Sloane 1952

Dumas, Vito *Alone Through the Roaring Forties* Harrap 1960;
    De Graff 1960

Gerbault, Alain *In Quest of the Sun* Hart-Davis 1955; Essential
    Books 1955
    The Fight of the Firecrest Hart-Davis 1955; Essential Books
    1955

Graham, Robin Lee *Dove* Angus & Robertson 1972; Bantam
1973

Guzzwell, John *Trekka Round the World* Adlard Coles 1963;
    De Graff 1964

Horie, Kenichi *Sailing Alone Across the Pacific.* Collins 1965;
    Tuttle 1964

Knox-Johnston, Robin *A World of My Own* Cassell 1969;
    Morrow 1970

Lewis, David *The Ship that would not Travel Due West* Temple
    Press 1961; Hart-Davis 1963; St Martin's Press 1962

MacGregor, J. *The Voyage Alone in the Yawl Rob Roy* Hart-
    Davis 1954; Fernhill 1954 (reprint of 1867 edition)

McMullen, R. T. *Down Channel* Hart-Davis 1949

Martyr, James Weston *The Southseaman* Hart-Davis 1957;
    Essential Books 1957

Mermod, Michel *The Voyage of the Geneve* John Murray 1973

Moitessier, Bernard *Th! Long Way* Adlard Coles 1974;
    Doubleday 1975

Pidgeon, Harry *Around the World Singlehanded* Hart-Davis
    1950

Ridler, Donald *Erik the Red* Kimber 1972

Robertson, Dougal *Survive the Savage Sea* Elek 1973; Praeger
    1973

Rose, Alec *My Lively Lady* Nautical Publications 1968;
    McKay 1969

Slocum, Joshua *Sailing Alone Around the World* Collier-
    Macmillan 1970; Dover 1969; Sheridan 1954

Smeaton, Miles *Once is Enough* Hart-Davis 1960; Norton 1969

Tabarly, Eric *Pen Duick* Arthaud, Paris 1970; Adlard Coles
    1971

Tambs, Erling *The Cruise of the Tedy* Hart Davis 1948
Tomalin, Nicholas, & Hall, Ron *The Strange Voyage of Donald
    Crowhurst* Hodder & Stoughton 1970; Stein & Day 1971
Woolass, Peter *Stelda, George and I* Arlington Books 1971

PICTURE CREDITS

*The author wishes to thank the following for their permission to
use illustrations in this book:*
Transworld/Observer Associated Press (Cover Picture): Beken
of Cowes: Camera Press: Jonathan Eastland/Ajax News
Service: Keystone Press: Mansell Collection: Mary Evans
Picture Library: Popperfoto: Radio Times Hulton Picture
Library: Syndication International: Topix.

Maps and diagrams by Peter Bridgewater

INDEX

208